The End of Money

The story of bitcoin, cryptocurrencies and the

blockchain revolution

The End of Money

The story of bitcoin, cryptocurrencies and the blockchain revolution

ADAM ROTHSTEIN
NEW SCIENTIST

New
Scientist

Also available
as an ebook

Contents

Series introduction

New Scientist's Instant Expert books shine light on the subjects that we all wish we knew more about: topics that challenge, engage enquiring minds and open up a deeper understanding of the world around us. *Instant Expert* books are definitive and accessible entry points for curious readers who want to know how things work and why. Look out for the other titles in the series:

Scheduled for publication in spring 2017:
How Your Brain Works
The Quantum World
Where the Universe Came From

Scheduled for publication in autumn 2017:
How Evolution Explains Everything About Life
Machines That Think
Why The Universe Exists
Your Conscious Mind

About the author

Adam Rothstein is a writer and theorist on tactical and strategic uses of technology, focusing on historical deployment and social effects. He is a chronicler of future technologies, and experiments with radio waves, media waves, and the rift between institutional and insurgent technological approaches. He writes for a variety of publications, and his book *Drone* was published in 2015 by Bloomsbury Publishing. He is on Twitter @interdome.

Introduction

Take out a piece of money. A banknote, made from paper and maybe some plastic, wrinkled from being shoved in pockets or wallets. You can exchange it for goods or services, or put it in the bank for a rainy day. You know how much it's worth. If you give it to someone else, they know too. It can't get much simpler than that, right?

Starting in 2008, money became more complicated. Something called 'cryptocurrency' was invented, and in a short span of time it swept into the global consciousness. The name of this cryptocurrency was bitcoin, and – depending on who you asked – it was either the brave new future of money or a menace to the world economy.

To the uninitiated, bitcoin can be baffling and even scary. What is it? Who controls it? Who uses it, and why? Lurid headlines about cybercrime, embezzlement, drug trafficking, money laundering, corruption, murder and even the overthrow of governments have tainted its reputation. There is an element of truth to that shady reputation.

But there is another side to the story too. Cryptocurrencies may really be the future of money, and there are many good reasons to think that would be an improvement on what we have now.

The core innovation of cryptocurrency is a technology called the blockchain. You're going to read a lot about that in this book. The blockchain promises to be a disruptive technology *in extremis*, capable of transforming not just how money works but many other things too, from the law to democracy.

After cryptocurrencies were released into the world, we began to consider money as a technology. And that technology is sweeping out widely into the future, catching millions upon its bleeding edge. On the way to those possible futures we'll encounter some near-future innovations, such as internet-aware appliances, decentralized banks, and even autonomous corporations.

This *Instant Expert* guide will introduce this new concept of money as a digital technology. It will paint the broad strokes of what a cryptocurrency is, how it came to be, and where the blockchain might be going next. Along the way, we'll travel from the dark alleys of the internet to the penthouses of global finance. We'll get into the details of cryptographic mathematics, and explore the often strange bitcoin subculture. We'll talk about what makes the money in our pockets, what makes the economies of nations, and about what might change these notions for good.

Predicting the future of money is like trying to get rich gambling on horse races. But by the end of this book, you'll be in as good a position as anyone to visualize what's coming over the horizon.

I
Bitcoin: The basics

What exactly is a bitcoin? How can you get hold of them? And what can you buy?

What exactly is bitcoin?

Bitcoin is a new type of **digital currency** called **crypto-currency**. It is not controlled by banks or backed by national governments, but is generated by a decentralized network of computers using software to solve mathematical problems. It relies on a cryptographic technology called a **blockchain**. It is the first and largest cryptocurrency, though there are now many cryptocurrencies in existence.

How do I use bitcoins?

Bitcoins are not physical entities. They are not minted into notes and coins like dollars or euros. Instead, bitcoins are stored in a digital file called a **wallet**. This wallet is used to send bit-coins to others, using software on a smartphone or computer.

How do I get bitcoins?

There are a number of ways. The first is by '**mining**' them. You can do this by setting your computer to carry out the crypto-graphic calculations needed to sustain the cryptocurrency. This earns a chance of winning a small quantity of bitcoins. This is how the cryptocurrency was originally distributed. Today, however, the mining competition is so fierce that earning any bitcoins this way is very difficult without a large investment. Alternatively, you could pay for 'cloud mining' services, where someone else does the mining for you.

Another way of getting bitcoins is in person from some-one who already has some. Services such as localbitcoins.com connect individuals looking to exchange bitcoins for traditional currency such as dollars or euro.

Another way to acquire bitcoins is via exchanges, which allow you to convert one currency – dollars, pounds, euros, yuan or bitcoins – into another, just like any other foreign currency exchange. Mt. Gox (see Chapter 7) was once the largest exchange worldwide until it collapsed in 2014. At the end of 2016, the largest exchange by trading volume was BitMEX.

More recently, services have opened up that allow customers to link their bank services to cryptocurrency-holding services, allowing them to deposit bitcoins and spend in local, traditional currency such as dollars or pounds, and vice versa. Two examples of services like these are Coinbase and Bitpay.

Lastly, a straightforward way to get bitcoins is to accept them in exchange for the sale of goods and services. Companies such as Stripe and Paymium offer services to help merchants accept cryptocurrencies in their businesses.

FIGURE I.I   The symbol for bitcoin was created by Satoshi Nakamoto soon after he invented the cryptocurrency

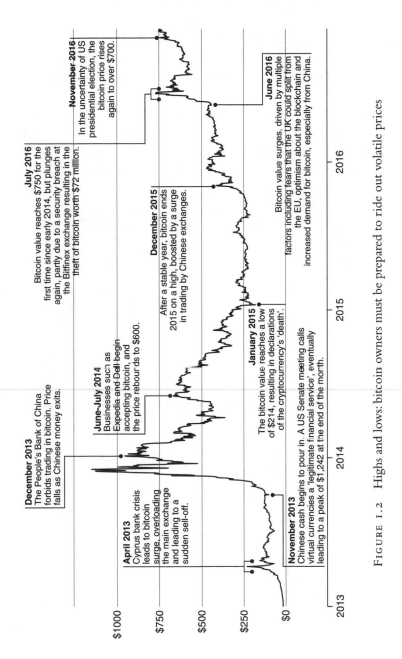

FIGURE 1.2   Highs and lows: bitcoin owners must be prepared to ride out volatile prices

December 2013
The People's Bank of China forbids trading in bitcoin. Price falls as Chinese money exits.

July 2016
Bitcoin value reaches $750 for the first time since early 2014, but plunges again, partly due to a security breach at the Bitfinex exchange resulting in the theft of bitcoin worth $72 million.

November 2016
In the uncertainty of US presidential election, the bitcoin price rises again to over $700.

April 2013
Cyprus bank crisis leads to bitcoin surge, overloading the main exchange and leading to a sudden sell-off.

June–July 2014
Businesses such as Expedia and Dell begin accepting bitcoin, and the price rebounds to $600.

December 2015
After a stable year, bitcoin ends 2015 on a high, boosted by a surge in trading by Chinese exchanges.

June 2016
Bitcoin value surges, driven by multiple factors including fears that the UK could split from the EU, optimism about the blockchain and increased demand for bitcoin, especially from China.

November 2013
Chinese cash begins to pour in. A US Senate meeting calls virtual currencies a 'legitimate financial service', eventually leading to a peak of $1,242 at the end of the month.

January 2015
The bitcoin value reaches a low of $214, resulting in declarations of the cryptocurrency's 'death'.

$1000
$750
$500
$250
$0

2013   2014   2015   2016

5

What can I buy with bitcoins?

In the early days of bitcoins, there wasn't much people could buy with them. The first major market that accepted bitcoin in payment traded in drugs and other illegal services. Today, many major businesses accept bitcoin directly, and for the dedicated bitcoin user, a card integration service like Coinbase or Bitpay allows customers to use bitcoins in any credit card transation.

2
The birth of bitcoin

In 2008, a person who did not exist had an idea. By 2011, that idea was worth over $54 million. This is the story of the invention of a radically new type of currency.

World-changing financial ideas don't usually appear out of the blue in email inboxes. So cryptographer Adam Back didn't pay much attention when he got an email from 'Satoshi **Nakamoto**' in August 2008 proposing a new idea for a **virtual currency**. Lots of people on the cypherpunk mailing list, which Back had followed since its creation in 1992, had proposed ideas for currencies that existed only within computers. Back didn't spend much time considering this particular concept, especially coming from an unknown name.

This was the first time anyone had heard from Nakamoto, a name believed to be made up by an unknown person or group. The idea – untested and unproven at that point – was called bitcoin. Less than three years later, when Satoshi Nakamoto disappeared from the internet, the total value of all bitcoin in existence was over $54.5 million. But the inventor of crypto-currency has never been positively identified.

The identity of bitcoin inventor 'Satoshi Nakamoto' is a mystery.

By the time Nakamoto disappeared, the code of his open-source software for this new type of currency had been rewritten so many times that it is difficult to say that Nakamoto is bitcoin's author. It is estimated that less than a third of bitcoin's com

$9.29 billion

Total value of all bitcoin in existence (August 2016)

puter code in use today was written by Nakamoto. Like so many other things that comprise the internet, the reality is that bitcoin now belongs to everyone and no one.

Strange ideas like bitcoin are common among the computer scientists, programmers, mathematicians and activists in the cypherpunk world, who have devised many complicated schemes to ensure technological privacy. Through experience, they are sceptical of ideas lauded as the 'next big thing'. So for a while, bitcoin seemed as if it might be yet another idea that would fall into obscurity. Bitcoin wasn't the first idea for a virtual currency, and none of the previous schemes had taken off.

Would the real Satoshi Nakamoto please stand up?

There have been many attempts to unveil the person behind the pseudonym of bitcoin's founder. All have failed.

- In October 2011, *New Yorker* journalist Joshua Davis suggests that computer scientist Michael Clear might be Satoshi, based on his background in **cryptography**, his use of vernacular British English, and his not-overt denial when first asked (he later denied it fully).

- The next day, magazine *Fast Company's* Adam L. Penenberg disagrees. He believes that Nakamoto must be one of three cryptographers – Neal King, Vladimir Oksman or Charles Bry – whose names appear on a cryptography patent filed three days before the first bitcoin.org website was registered by Nakamoto. But these connections turn out to be coincidences.
- Users on a bitcoin forum suggest in 2012 that **Jed McCaleb**, founder of the bitcoin exchange Mt. Gox, might be Satoshi.
- Postings in other forums around this time suggest the conspiracy theory that bitcoin might have been founded by the US Central Intelligence Agency or National Security Agency, to lure in unsuspecting criminals.
- In 2013, after the arrest of Ross Ulbricht, founder of the illicit dark web shopping site Silk Road, two Israeli researchers conclude that Ulbricht must be Nakamoto.
- In March 2014, *Newsweek* reporter Leah McGrath Goodman drops the bombshell claim that the real name of the creator of bitcoin *is* Satoshi Nakamoto, though he goes by the first name, Dorian. She bases her claim on Dorian Nakamoto's programming experience, and his long time residence in Silicon Valley.
- In the widespread debunking of the Dorian Nakamoto claim, *Forbes* writer Andy Greenberg investigates the possibility that bitcoin code-contributor Hal Finney is the real Nakamoto, but soon rejects the idea.
- Nathaniel Popper's 2015 book, *Digital Gold,* suggests that Nick Szabo – Cypherpunk, bitcoin investor, and inventor of the earlier virtual currency, BitGold – is Satoshi Nakamoto. Szabo publicly denies the claim.

- In late 2015, *Wired* magazine and online site *Gizmodo* get a tip and a trove of leaked documents that point to Australian programmer Craig Wright. He initially denies it, but in the spring of 2016 Wright then claims that he is Nakamoto, and that he created bitcoin along with his since-deceased associate Dave Kleiman. Although he is able to present a significant amount of proof, it is not enough to satisfy many sceptics, and so the mystery lingers still. (For more on this, see Chapter 10.)

The first bitcoin

Nakamoto didn't give up after one email. After contacting Back, Nakamoto posted his idea to a public email list about cryptography. Next, he posted it on a website called the P2P Foundation, which accepted submissions of all kinds of peer-to-peer technology projects. One person who thought the idea had some merit was Hal Finney, a programmer who had worked on **Pretty Good Privacy**, a free encryption software. Intrigued by the distributed, cryptographic aspects of bitcoin, Finney worked with Nakamoto on the code. He also received the first bitcoin ever sent, from Nakamoto in early 2009. It was worth a pittance then.

Slowly and surely, bitcoin began to take off. Two budding programmers, Gavin Andresen and Martti Malmi, liked the idea and helped Nakamoto build a website and improve the bitcoin code. They invented the term 'cryptocurrency' to describe a virtual currency built around cryptography. They set up a forum in the autumn of 2009 for the nascent community of cryptography geeks, libertarians and programmers who were interested in the strange possibility that an idea for a decentralized currency might actually work.

The more the developers tweaked the code, experimented with it, and ran it through its paces, the more it seemed like it could become more than just an idea. The code worked. It was resilient. As more people downloaded the software and set their computers to perform the tasks necessary to generate the currency, the more solid it appeared.

If the technical aspects of bitcoin were looking good, other aspects were still lacking. By the beginning of 2010, there was still no good way to buy bitcoins, nor anything to buy with them – there were just a few small websites that sold a selection of bitcoin goods, such as stickers and T-shirts. There was one famous incident in April 2010 when an enthusiast named Laszlo Hanyecz got someone in the forum to send two pizzas to his house in exchange for 10,000 bitcoins, but that was hardly a reliable means of ordering pizza.

Going viral

In July 2010, the popular tech news aggregator, Slashdot, bumped a story about bitcoin to its front page. Downloads of the program jumped nearly sevenfold. Bitcoin was going viral, but there was still no way for all these interested people to get hold of any.

The bitcoin network distributes new bitcoins in return for performing tricky 'proof-of-work' calculations (see Chapter 4). In those early days, when a computer running the software solved one of these 'blocks', it got a reward for the effort; 50 new bitcoins were created and added to the user's virtual wallet (see 'The world of currency mining', Chapter 5). This also solved the problem of where the money 'comes from', because there is no central bank to distribute it.

Back when there were only a few computers on the network, claiming this reward wasn't hard. Since Satoshi Nakamoto's computer was often the only one on the network for most of the cryptocurrency's first year, his wallet accumulated an estimated one million bitcoins in block rewards. But as more and more people started running the software, the **difficulty** of solving blocks increased (see 'A digital arms race', Chapter 5). There were so many people doing the proof-of-work, it became rare for an individual computer plugged into the network to win a block. It was almost like winning a lottery.

At this point, bitcoins were still very cheap. When individuals traded them for cash, they were worth only a few cents each. These trades were done on an ad hoc basis, in forums and by email. If there was no system to readily get hold of even a few dollars' worth of bitcoins, how would anyone ever be able to use them as a currency? People needed to be able to buy them in quantity at market rates, and they had to be accepted in trade for goods.

Does it matter who Satoshi is?

The identity of bitcoin's founder is one of the biggest mysteries of the internet. But does it matter who he or she really is?

Not only is Satoshi Nakamoto a historical figure, responsible for the creation of a massive digital storehouse of value, but he likely controls a significant part of that value. Experts estimate that the bitcoin he owns is worth over $600 million dollars. And regardless of the exchange value, that currency will be nearly 5 per cent of the total cryptocurrency in the bitcoin system, once it reaches full capacity. Whoever controls that portion of the cryptocurrency, certainly wields a substantial amount of power over it.

But many proponents of cryptocurrencies are happy that he has never been conclusively identified. Without a founder, there is no Henry Ford or Steve Jobs, no major

---

figure to deliver pronouncements about the direction that development should take. Instead, anyone who can come up with an idea is just as capable of pursuing it and selling it to the public at large.

This doesn't stop the insatiable curiosity about Satoshi's identity. It is rare to have a public figure so shrouded in mystery, who just disappears without a trace. What does he think about the development of cryptocurrencies? Where did the idea come from? What sort of things is he doing now? It is possible we will never know.

The exchange

Among the many people who discovered bitcoin was Jed McCaleb, co-creator of the peer-to-peer file-sharing program, eDonkey. Using an old domain name from an abandoned project related to the *Magic: The Gathering* card game, he started a bitcoin exchange called Mt. Gox. There, anyone could buy and sell bitcoins for real US dollars, in a price that fluctuated according to market demand. With the added publicity from Slashdot, Mt. Gox took off as the first real cryptocurrency exchange.

It was now possible to buy bitcoins for dollars. But there was still nothing to buy with them. That changed in the beginning of 2011 due to two events.

In December 2010, after whistleblower website WikiLeaks leaked classified information from the US government

$0.08
Price of bitcoin after Mt. Gox exchange opens (July 2010)

to the internet, PayPal and other payment processors refused to process donations to WikiLeaks. Libertarians, cypherpunks, and internet activists decried this as censorship, and bitcoin was discussed as a potential solution to this problem. Without a company controlling bitcoin, users could make all the donations they wished, and there would be no one the government could force to implement an embargo of WikiLeaks. The price of a bitcoin on Mt. Gox rose to 30 cents that month with the hype.

The marketplace

Two months later, another idealist decided to put bitcoin's ability to bypass government influence to the test. A person who identified himself only as 'Dread Pirate Roberts' started a website called **Silk Road**, the goal of which was to create an Amazon-like marketplace for illicit and illegal products, with a general ideology of thwarting government control. Taking a philosophy of only selling 'victimless products' (drugs and forged government documents were okay while weapons, illegal pornography, and stolen identities were not allowed), the site was visible only to users connecting with the address-anonymizing software called **TOR**. This masked zone is known as the **dark web**. And the only currency accepted on Silk Road was bitcoin.

The increased anonymity offered by bitcoin over credit card transactions meant that internet-savvy drug traffickers

$1242

Highest price of bitcoin in history (November 2013)

You don't need physical coins to use bitcoin, but some physical tokens
have been created.

gave Silk Road a shot, despite its vulnerabilities. The site was
so popular that it shut down several times during the first half
of 2011, unable to deal with the traffic. An article on the now
defunct website *Gawker* about Silk Road was published in June
of that year. Immediately, Silk Road's business boomed. Now
with something, albeit illegal, for people to buy with bitcoin, the
price for one bitcoin on Mt. Gox rose from a price of around
70 cents in February 2011, to nearly $10 in May, and $32 in
mid-June.

The Silk Road boom brought other unde-sired public attention to bitcoin. On 5 June 2011, US Senator Chuck Sch-

$450 million

Value of bitcoin stolen in Mt. Gox collapse (February 2014)

umer held a press conference at which he denounced bitcoin and Silk Road, and pressed federal authorities to crack down. The US Drug Enforcement Administration and the Justice Department issued press releases expressing their concern. In June, Dread Pirate Roberts voluntarily put Silk Road on hiatus, hoping that the heat would die down.

With bitcoin's rising notoriety, others tried to distance themselves from it. Jed McCaleb, the founder of Mt. Gox, was becoming overwhelmed by the stress of guarding the site from hackers. One such attack broke into the site and spirited away $45,000 worth of bitcoins in January 2011. In March, McCaleb sold the site to another developer.

It was during this time, in April 2011, that developers of bit-coin software heard the last of Satoshi Nakamoto. After some terse email exchanges in which Nakamoto expressed concern about the negative press that came with these anti-government causes, as well as worries about his pseudonym becoming something of a notorious legend among bitcoin proponents, the creator of the first cryptocurrency signed off. The forum username went dark, and the emails stopped coming. The anonymous creator of bitcoin simply ceased to exist.

But there was too much money at stake for bitcoin to disappear. At the time Nakamoto disappeared the total value of all bitcoin in existence was around $54.5 million. Just two months later that had increased to more than $207 million. During a trading peak of 2.8 million bitcoins exchanged on 8 June 2011, Mt. Gox had earned around $900,000 in commissions over a 24-hour period. After Dread Pirate Roberts turned his site on again in July, Silk Road was generating commissions of $30,000 a month, and that number was quickly rising. Cryptocurrency was no longer just an idea. The nebulous, internet-dream quality of it evaporated along with its supposed creator, and what was left was real money, with real value – and all the problems that come with it.

3
How to create a currency, the crypto way

An unlikely mix of hackers and spies developed the technology that allowed bitcoin to exist. They created secret communication channels and dark shadow networks on an otherwise easily trackable internet.

Bitcoin, the first cryptocurrency, did not just spontaneously appear. Many of the technologies it is built on are at least as old as the internet itself. The roots of cryptocurrency's underlying blockchain technology go deep into a community of hackers, activists and technologists who still influence the development and direction of cryptocurrencies, and the internet at large, today.

An essential tool within bitcoin is digital cryptography. This crucial component of the internet is present in everything from WiFi to email, digital shopping carts to credit cards. Without cryptography to keep information private online, there would be no internet as we know it. And without cryptography, cryptocurrencies could not function.

Digital cryptographic tools have long been the province of characters on the fringes of society: hackers and spies. At first glance these two groups might not seem to have much in common, but both share a need for absolute privacy.

Between the two poles of hackers and spies lies the dark web – the part of the internet hidden from prying eyes by encryption. The dark web pushes the boundary of what is possible, as well as what is legal. It is here that the idea of cryptocurrency was born. Indeed, it could not have been born anywhere else.

The birth of cypherpunk

In 1970s a US counter-cultural group called the Yippies, led by activist Abbie Hoffman, began publishing a newsletter that taught, among other tricks, how to steal service from telephone service providers. What began as an anti-authority gesture evolved into something more. Self-described 'hackers' began experimenting to see just how far they could break into technological systems without getting caught.

But once the technology evolved and phone lines became data lines, this exploration became more serious. Actions once considered pranks or victimless theft soon became real disruptions. In 1988, a computer worm that would come to be called the Morris Worm began replicating itself across computers via the internet. The self-replicating malware's intent wasn't to break anything, but simply to spread as far as it could. But in the process of doing so, it crashed many systems. The US authorities did not find this experiment amusing. Robert Morris, a graduate student and creator of the Morris Worm, became the first person convicted under the Computer Fraud and Abuse Act for intentionally accessing federal computers (where his worm eventually ended up) without authorization, and for causing significant damage.

As the internet developed and computers became increasingly networked, hackers came up against more legal obstacles. In the 1990s, governments around the world began to take action, attempting to tame the lawless internet. In response, sections of the computer community took counteraction. Some were motivated by libertarian and anarchist philosophies, united by their general distrust of government. Others, seeing how law enforcement agencies could persecute those who didn't mean any real harm, began organizing to defend radical hackers and everyday computer users alike. In 1990, the Electronic Frontier Foundation was created in response to the ongoing computer crime crackdown. This non-profit organization still exists today, providing legal counsel and activism on a wide variety of pro-privacy issues. But computer users needed more than lawyers to defend themselves against the government's move into the internet. They needed new technology.

The early 1990s gave birth to the 'cypherpunk' − a type of hacker whose bread and butter was digital cryptography.

The cypherpunks didn't focus on breaking into computer systems. Rather, they developed tools that created a shroud of electronic privacy on the internet.

The digital privacy tools created by 'cypherpunks' helped give rise to cryptocurrencies

The most important tool evolved from a discovery by scientists Whitfield Diffie and Martin Hellman in 1976. They figured out a method of asymmetric encryption (see 'Public-key encryption', Chapter 4) that allowed two people to communicate secretly, without ever having to exchange a code book. In 1991, adapting this technique to the internet age, software engineer and anti-nuclear activist Phil Zimmerman developed a program called Pretty Good Privacy (PGP) and uploaded the source code to the internet where anyone could download it and send encrypted messages for free. The cypherpunks were ecstatic. The software worked so well for keeping communications secret that the US government attempted to prosecute Zimmerman for 'exporting a munition': a violation of laws attempting to keep technology with high military value from leaving the country.

One year later, in September 1992, an online mailing list was launched under the name Cypherpunk. The conversation attracted all sorts of people interested in using technology to maintain their privacy, and included such tools as PGP, remailing services that obscured an email sender's true address, and hypothetical ideas such as 'untraceable' digital money.

At that time, with the government after Zimmerman, it was not clear that encryption would be legal in the long run. The Cypherpunk list, therefore, attracted people not only interested in privacy but also those willing to stray into the grey areas of the law in order to protect their privacy. The cypherpunks thought it likely that if they did not push the technological envelope, the new internet would be used entirely for surveillance, and personal privacy might be lost forever. They began to consider their actions, like those of Zimmerman, to be civil disobedience – releasing information to the public for the public's good, regardless of what the government said was legal.

Virtual currency proponents were on the Cypherpunk list from the very beginning. Hal Finney, who worked on PGP with Phil Zimmerman, was on the list and would later be one of the first to help Satoshi Nakamoto improve the bitcoin source code. Another person on the list was Adam Back, who used cryptography to develop a spam reduction tool called 'hashcash', which he shared with the Cypherpunk email list in 1997. Also on the list were cryptographer Nick Szabo who experimented with a virtual currency of his own, called Bit Gold, and Craig Wright, an Australian involved in various security technologies, including those securing financial transactions. All of these names would be important in the future of bitcoin and cryptocurrencies.

In 2008, Satoshi Nakamoto publicly announced his idea for a cryptocurrency he called 'bitcoin' on a successor mailing list to Cypherpunk's original email list. Although many were initially sceptical about bitcoin's efficacy, Nakamoto had found the ideal audience to appreciate his concept.

But cypherpunks are only half the history of the dark web. The other half comes from a tool developed by the US authorities to protect their spies.

Spies who logged on in the dark

In 1995, the concept of 'onion routing' was invented by Paul Syverson, Michael Reed and David Goldschlag who worked at the US Office of Naval Research. They were funded by the Defense Advanced Research Projects Agency (DARPA), which developed new technologies for the military. Their goal wasn't to avoid government surveillance – on the contrary, they were trying to enable it.

The internet works via a connected group of dedicated computers called 'routers'. When computer A wants to communicate with computer B, it sends a packet of information from one internet protocol (IP) address to another. All the routers process this address and make sure that the packet of information travels across this web of wires to its desired destination.

The problem is that any computer along the way can see the addresses of both computer A and computer B by looking at the data packet. It's like looking at a letter in someone's mailbox. You might not be able to read the message inside the envelope (especially if that message is encrypted), but you can still read the destination and return addresses on the envelope, which must be written in clear text for the mail carrier to deliver it.

THE END OF MONEY

In this state of affairs, if a US spy is undercover they can't communicate with a computer back at Naval Intelligence headquarters without giving themselves away. The same conundrum applies to the officer sitting at a desk at Naval Intelligence headquarters who is trying to investigate a terrorist message board. Going 'undercover' on the internet is nearly impossible if your adversary knows how to look for the data packets' addresses. All the packets eventually trace back to their source.

The onion routing concept solved this problem in the form of software called 'Tor'. Tor creates an anonymous network by covering up the packets' addresses with a series of encrypted 'layers', like an onion skin. Between computer A and B, internet traffic is routed around a series of encrypted connections, each forming another layer. Before the data packet is inside the Tor network, it is impossible to tell its ultimate destination. When it comes out the other side, it is impossible to tell where it came from. Onion routing doesn't encrypt the traffic itself, but obscures its origin and destination and makes it, for all intents and purposes, untraceable.

Is cryptography only for people with something to hide?

Encryption isn't just for cypherpunks and spies anymore. Every digital service we use employs encryption to scramble the information to give us some privacy online. It protects our medical records, bank data and messages that we send over the internet.

Given how many of our conversations and information channels use digital systems, the likelihood that someone might be trying to eavesdrop on us is growing. That is why every digital service uses encryption to help protect

---

us, to give us that privacy we have come to expect. But not all standard encryption is equal. Some of it is easily broken. Some of it has holes. That is why many people are now taking the technology into their own hands, learning to use cryptographic technologies such as Tor, and **public-key encryption.**

This works well for spies but it is also great for activists who don't want to be spied on by their governments. Ironically, the government dropped the project development in 2004 and made it open source. It was quickly supported by the Electronic Frontier Foundation, which helped the independent, non-profit Tor Project (that still develops the software today) get started. Today, many people use Tor software to hide their internet traffic from prying eyes of all kinds.

It might seems odd that spies and hackers use the same tool. Many conspiracy theorists believe, therefore, that Tor might be a trick propagated by the US government. But what they fail to understand is that spies and hackers have the same goal – to mask their activities online within a dark web.

Tor also allows what are called 'hidden services'. When a website **server** is connected to Tor, only computers that are connected to Tor are allowed to load the website. Rather than using Tor to connect to the regular internet, this is a separate 'mini-internet' that is only visible inside the onion-routing-network. This means that everything which happens on that hidden service site, when configured correctly, is anonymous. No one can tell where the server or the site's viewers are located. A site like this is referred to as being part of the 'dark web'.

In the dark web, a person could just as easily be a cop as a Cypherpunk anarchist. That's both the problem and the benefit of anonymity – you can't tell who anyone really is. And it was in this cypherpunk-descended anonymity that cryptocurrencies were born and raised.

What did the random shopper bot buy on the dark web?

Carmen Weisskopf is part of !Mediengruppe Bitnik, a group of artists who work on and with the internet. She gave a software bot some bitcoins and sent it shopping in the dark side of the internet – where it bought things that no bot has bought before.

Tell me about your art project to use a bot to randomly shop on the dark net.

The Random Darknet Shopper is a bot programmed to shop in the deep web or dark net once a week, with a maximum budget of $100 in bitcoins.

What exactly are the deep web and dark net?

The deep web is part of the internet comprised of all the web pages that aren't indexed by search engines, such as intranets. It's actually larger than the 'surface web' that most people are used to. Part of the deep web is encrypted and accessed through TOR browsers to hide where you come from. This is called the dark net.

What has your bot bought from the dark net?

Most items there have dubious legal status. In 2014 when we tried it we got a set of master keys used by firefighters, cigarettes, fake jeans and trainers, some ebooks, a credit card, a scan of a passport and some ecstasy. That was the first time a bot had bought drugs. It raises the question of who is responsible for a bot's actions.

What did your shopper bot buy when you set it off again?

Some firecrackers, a fake Lacoste shirt and two USB devices to mine bitcoins. It chose these items randomly, but it did seem like the bot was saying: 'OK you're not giving me enough money to spend'.

How do you feel as you open up the unknown parcels delivered from the dark net?

It's always exciting, but it's also scary to run the bot and to see what it will buy. We're hoping for a diverse set of items that give a good insight into the dark net landscape.

Does anything go? What if your bot bought a bomb-making kit?

$100 in bitcoins doesn't buy that much. This ensures the items remain manageable. Also, there aren't that many items that fill us with fear on these deep web markets.

Why would you want to randomly shop for things in the dark net? Isn't it a haven for illegal stuff?

So is the surface web! This project started out with the Snowden revelations. It made us re-evaluate mass surveillance of the surface web, where everyone who uses it is trackable. So we started looking at the dark net, where encryption is built in. It is a necessity for people to remain anonymous in certain situations. We started thinking about how trust is formed in an anonymous network. And we wanted to know what was actually sold and bought there.

What about trust? Has the bot been scammed yet, and paid for goods that haven't been delivered?

No. And this shows the level of trust that is there. The people who sell on these markets are used to trusting people online, and want to get a good rating. Even the Swiss police who seized the ecstasy bought by our bot were surprised at its quality compared to that available on the streets.

Interview by Alison George for New Scientist *magazine.*

4
The blockchain

If money goes digital, how do you stop it from being replicated? Currency that's just as easy to copy as a digital file would be completely worthless. The solution is a cunning cryptographic ledger called the blockchain.

The blockchain, Satoshi Nakamoto's innovation, is the heart and soul of cryptocurrencies. It sets cryptocurrencies apart from other digital or virtual currencies. It secures the cryptocurrency by, among other things, making it impossible for someone to counterfeit bitcoin – no easy task. This innovation is arguably the main reason why bitcoin has succeeded where other virtual currencies have failed. Traditional currencies rely on producing notes that are certified and tracked by an official source, such as a bank or a treasury. They make it as difficult as possible to produce counterfeits and so people trust the value of the currency. Things aren't so easy in the digital world.

Any attempt to create digital currency is immediately faced with a problem. Any digital file can easily be replicated. If anyone can replicate the file representing digital currency, then it becomes easily counterfeited, and then it is worthless. But this isn't only a problem for digital currencies – record labels, book publishers, film studios, and even fashion labels of the 21st century are all facing similar issues.

Those industries know that if anybody can reproduce their own copy of a film, book, or fabric pattern, then few people would actually bother to pay for it. So to try to counteract this trend many companies have started using Digital Rights Management (DRM) software. The software helps to prevent people from sharing copies of digital files by checking with a central server to see whether the person using the file is known to have paid for it. For example, if you go to watch a film on your computer the DRM software will consult a central server to see if you purchased it from a registered outlet. If you did, the file is then unlocked and you can begin watching the film; if not then you are blocked from watching it.

But this solution is not perfect. Servers can break down or be shut down, leaving those who paid for the media in a worse

THE END OF MONEY

position than those who pirated it. Electronic banking technology is similar. When logging in to a bank account, a form
of digital currency, we use the internet to access the bank's
computer where our records are stored and certified – but if
the bank's system goes down, there is no access to the money.
Other attempts to utilize digital and virtual currencies before
bitcoin worked this way, in that they relied upon central companies to hold and authenticate all the records. When those
companies failed, the currencies disappeared.

The blockchain changed everything. In the simplest terms,
the blockchain is just a ledger that lists all of the units of the
cryptocurrency and who owns them. As money changes hands,
the ledger is rewritten to reflect the transaction. This way, it
doesn't matter where the money is physically located as long as
there is a single list of all the units in existence, and who owns
how much. If you tried to replicate digital coins you would
soon be found out when you went to spend them, as they
wouldn't be accounted for in the blockchain.

The blockchain means that bitcoins never actually need to
exist. No one actually 'sends' the coins anywhere. They just
update the blockchain to reflect who owns what. The currency
is basically one giant list of IOUs. Any attempts to tamper with
the currency can be easily detected by checking the blockchain. It is an ingeniously elegant solution to a problem that
many people thought would never be solved.

Public-key encryption

The blockchain is run on encryption – hence the name 'cryptocurrency'. Contemporary encryption uses what is called asymmetric, or 'public-key', encryption, just like PGP (see 'The
birth of Cypherpunk', Chapter 3). A crucial difference from

other encryption methods is that, from a mathematical standpoint, the decryption process is not simply the reverse of the encryption process: hence the term asymmetric.

Public-key encryption is based on the principle that there are mathematical problems which are much easier to solve forwards than backwards. For example, multiplying two six-digit prime numbers like 323,123 and 596,977 together is a relatively easy task. With a minute and a pencil and paper, you would get 192,896,999,171. But if instead you were given the number 192,896,999,171 and asked to find the two prime numbers that divide it, you would need a lot more time to test all of the different possibilities. In public-key encryption the numbers are much larger, but computers have to perform very similar tasks.

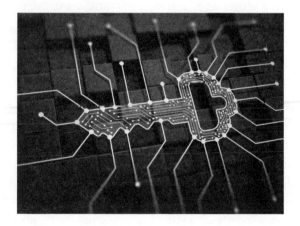

Public-key encryption keeps online information away from prying eyes.

A user has two keys: a public key used to encrypt messages, and a private key to decrypt them. The private key might consist of very large prime numbers (hundreds or thousands of digits long), and the public key the result of multiplying them together.

The private key is used to generate the public key, and this generation process can be verified, meaning that the two keys are forever linked together. A user can be confident that they can share the public key with anyone without anyone discovering their private key, as it's very difficult to reverse the generation process.

Using the public key anyone can encrypt a message, but the private key is required to decrypt it. Suppose you want to send a friend an encrypted message. Here's the procedure:

1 Your friend uses their private key to generate a public key, which they can share with anyone. They send a copy of it to you.
2 You encrypt a message using their public key and then send the message to them. Anyone who intercepts the message won't be able to read it, as they don't have the private key. This includes you – the encryption process only works one direction.
3 Your friend receives the message and uses their private key to decrypt it.

As long as no one but your friend has the private key, a message encrypted with their public key will never be read by anyone other than them.

Public-key encryption is so strong that the only way for most users to try to break through encryption is called the 'brute-force' method. That means trying every possible secret key until you hit the right one. Literally, guessing at computer speed. Researchers are currently using a faster way, called 'factorization', to shortcut the mathematics, but it is still very slow.

One type of public-key encryption commonly used today is called RSA after the inventors – Rivest, Shamir and Adleman. In 2009, researchers were able to use a series of supercomputers working on a factorization method to break a 768-bit key, but it took them two years. The next strongest key length in use is 1024-bit and was estimated by the same researchers to take 1000 times longer to crack. No one has done it yet, as far as we know. The strongest key length currently in use for RSA is 4096-bit. Researchers estimate that the amount of time required to break a key of that length, using today's highest tech, would be 'practically infinite'.

Cryptographically sign on the dotted line

It's important to know that you're not being deceived, especially on the internet. If Microsoft sends you an update how do you know the new software is actually from them and hasn't been switched to a computer virus? Or if you receive an email from a friend, how do you know it hasn't been intercepted and edited before getting to you? The answer is digital **signatures**.

Digital signatures use similar concepts to public-key cryptography. They employ short strings of unique characters called a **hash**. Using a private key, a message is reduced to this hash. The hashing process can be verified with a public key. But changing the original message, even by one character, would completely alter the hash in an unpredictable way. You can use this method to sign a message, so the recipient knows that it was sent by you, exactly as it is, without any changes or deletions.

1 Take the message you want to sign and using your private key, sign the message and create a unique hash.
2 Encrypt the message with a friend's public key, and send the encrypted message to a friend. They decrypt the message using their private key.

> 3 Your friend uses your public key to inspect the hash. They
>   see that indeed, this message could only have been signed
>   with your private key and that the message is exactly the
>   same as the one you used to generate the hash.
>
> Digital signatures can be used to verify that messages
> match the original. But their use is even more wide-
> ranging than that. They also can verify that downloaded
> files match the source, provide digital 'handshakes' for
> secure connections to servers, and maintain a chain of
> custody for digital documents.

How does the blockchain store transactions?

The blockchain is like a digital ledger, a long list of IOUs, that
tracks the changes in ownership of each bitcoin. The blockchain verifies all the **transactions** that are added to it, using
a method similar to public key cryptography and signatures
(see 'Public-key encryption' and 'Cryptographically sign on the
dotted line', above). However, because it is meant for financial
transactions, the terminology differs a little.

Your 'wallet' functions like a private key. It is secret, known
only by you, and is the link between all of the bitcoins you
own. Your 'address' functions like a public key. It is generated by
your wallet, and can be given freely to anyone, who can now
send you bitcoins. Your wallet can also digitally sign your transactions, sent to the blockchain.

Here is a step-by-step breakdown of a bitcoin transaction.
It's very similar to sending a message using encryption.

1 You get the digital address of a friend to whom you
   would like to send some bitcoins.

2 You send a transaction to the blockchain. The transaction consists of your address, how many coins you would like to send, the digital addresses of your friend, and your digital signature.

3 Upon receiving the message, the blockchain verifies that the bitcoin associated with your address has enough of a balance to send the coins, and that your digital signature is valid. If everything is OK the blockchain is updated, now showing the transfer between you and your friend. This transaction is signed by the blockchain itself, which registers it as official and valid.

There is no limit to the number of public keys a wallet can create. So the amount of coins associated with one wallet might be logged to any number of public keys in the blockchain. It's a bit like one person having several different bank accounts, or one building having many different post boxes. The wallet always remains private, but anyone can see the public keys in the blockchain. In the blockchain is the entire record of where every coin has been, as it has bounced around from address to address, split into pieces, transferred, combined, and then split again. Even though this is a long, complex series of transfers, it can be analysed and the money can be followed around the ledger.

The wallet, i.e. the private key, is the only identity required to enter a transaction from one address to another. As long as the wallet is safe and only under your control, you are the only one who can move your bitcoins. The fact that next to every transaction recorded in the blockchain is a digital signature associated with the address, means that anyone can check the validity of a transaction. Every transaction that has ever happened is contained within the blockchain, and every computer can check all the signatures going back through the recorded history, to prove the continuity.

The blockchain is the place where all transactions are certified, but it in itself needs to be verified as true and consistent. The worry is not so much of attackers sending false transactions to move other people's bitcoins – the wallet's signatures protect against that. The problem is more about transactions being deleted or undone. If someone had the power to unilaterally edit the ledger, turning back time and undoing previous transactions, then they would also have the power to create bitcoins out of thin air by restoring them to previous owners who had already exchanged them. The solution is to make sure that no individual has this control of the blockchain, by making sure that everyone does.

The blockchain is the tool that underlies cryptocurrency

A place to keep the ledger

The blockchain is everywhere. Every computer running the cryptocurrency downloads its own copy of an identical ledger from the other computers in the network. As each computer adds transactions to the blockchain, it simultaneously updates the network by bouncing the information around to the other computers. The idea is that if any one person attempts to alter the blockchain's transaction history, it would no longer match all the other copies.

But then new transactions present a problem. If someone creates two new, contradicting transactions, how will the blockchain know which one to trust? Altering the entire history of the blockchain would be obvious, but small erroneous additions and subtractions submitted to the blockchain could quickly add up. If I tell one computer in the network that I will give a coin to one friend, and I tell another computer in the network that I will give the same coin to a different friend, which transaction is correct? The problem of all digital assets exists – transactions could be, in effect, duplicated. In cryptocurrencies, this problem is called double-spending.

Across the worldwide span of the network, different versions of the ledger might exist, with contradictions, or attempts to fool the network into thinking coins are assigned to two different places at once. How would the differences be resolved? How could you use this system as currency, if a customer leaves with a product, but then 30 minutes later the merchant discovers the coins they thought they had received had actually been sent elsewhere, or maybe back to the customer themselves? The blockchain employs an ingenious solution.

Proof-of-work

Bitcoin, and all the cryptocurrencies that were developed directly from its model, ensure there is only one, canonical ledger, with no contradictions, by using a technique called 'proof-of-work'. This allows the blockchain to be stored on every computer in the network at the same time, but also ensure that each copy of the blockchain will be identical.

As long as the blockchain is ensured to be consistent and identical across all versions, the bitcoins can be trusted as currency even though they are entirely virtual. All duplicate and erroneous transactions are weeded out, and each bitcoin can only be held by one owner at one time – eliminating the double-spending problem.

A proof-of-work task is based on the same mathematics used in public-key cryptography – though its process is separate from the cryptography used in transactions. The idea was suggested in 1997 by programmer Adam Back for a system called hashcash. Back's idea was a computer having to complete a difficult task that took, for example, ten minutes, before it could send an email. For a person sending 50 emails a day the prerequisite would be trivial, limiting them to one email every ten minutes. But for a spammer who wanted to send thousands and thousands of emails a day, it would make widespread spamming impossible.

A timer could be circumvented perhaps, but for a computer a task is a more firm limit. Computers are designed to solve long series of tasks quickly. However, a scalable series of tasks, such as those involving cryptography, can easily be scaled up to take exponentially longer on more powerful machines. A task of variable difficulty can be scaled on the fly to make sure that no matter what computer was working on it, from a cellphone to a supercomputer, the task would take roughly the same amount of time. It is like moving the finish line of a race so that a car finishes exactly at a specific time, no matter how fast or slow the car drives.

No shortcut

If the task involves cryptography, then there is no shortcut. A proof-of-work task can only be completed by 'brute force'.

The task, in this case, is an attempt to generate the correct hash as if for a signature, but without using a private key – instead by trying lots of different possible hashes, simply by guessing, until it finds the right one.

In effect, the proof-of-work problem is like brute-forcing a low-level cryptographic signature, for which a secret key never existed. The cryptography is scaled down a great deal from commonly used cryptography, so that the computer network can actually solve the problem in ten minutes. A computer can make thousands of guesses per second. The network can make quadrillions of guesses per second. As more computers connect into the network, they each begin working on the same proof-of-work problem, which would ordinarily shorten the time until the solution is reached. But the 'difficulty' of the proof-of-work is adjusted automatically so that each solution always takes ten minutes, regardless of how many computers are generating hash guesses.

Once a computer thinks it has the right hash for the cryptographic mathematical problem, another computer in the network can verify this quickly. Verification is a snap, compared to guessing over and over again. But because no secret key exists, guessing and verifying is the only way to come up with this correct hash. That is why it is called 'proof-of-work'. There is no solution other than proving you did the brute-force work.

Cryptocurrencies that rely on proof-of-work use this sort of time limit to determine the length of time that the block is 'open' for transactions, before it is written to the blockchain. When the proof-of-work is complete, the block is closed. Bitcoin is designed so that each block takes about ten minutes to solve, but the time varies with other cryptocurrencies.

Proof-of-work might sound like a very roundabout way of making the block close every ten minutes, but there is an important reason for it. During the ten minutes of the bitcoin block duration, the network shares all the transactions to be added to the blockchain among all its computers. The network has a chance to compare all new transactions, and delete the duplicates or contradicting transactions. This is the first barrier to any sort of double-spending transactions.

The computer that finds the solution to the proof-of-work problem will be, effectively, chosen at random due to the brute-force method of the proof-of-work. This computer is said to have 'solved' the block. Only the transactions received by the computer that solves the block are included. Any transactions that didn't make the cut-off must wait for the next block. This randomization also helps prevent against double-spending transactions. If it is impossible to predict where the block will be solved, it is more difficult to attempt to game the system.

The actual data of the block contains not only those transactions and the proof-of-work solution, but also includes the hash of the block that came before it. The new block is 'signed' in this way by using the previous block, and so on, all the way back to the beginning. This has the added benefit of recertifying historical transactions every time a new block is formed. If the information in any previous block is changed even just by one character, it will change the signature, which will change the next block, and the next, and so on. Therefore, the historical blockchain cannot be altered, without changing every block down the line. The blocks are immutably linked together, and means that the current block is always a unique product of all those that came before it, and nothing can be inserted in the middle.

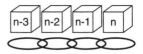

FIGURE 4.1 The *blockchain* is a series of *blocks*.

No false information

To add false information or remove transactions from a previous block, one would have to recreate all the blocks from the desired change point forward, including the new block that is currently being solved, in order to redo the signatures all the way back up the chain. It would be like a runner stopping a race in the middle, returning to the start line, and then running fast enough to catch the runners who had never stopped. The only way that a computer could win this race is if it were producing hash guesses faster than all the other computers combined. This also protects against double-spending, by making it impossible to reverse previous transactions by simply removing them from the blockchain.

In addition to this complicated signing and hashing serving to lock each block to the next in the chain, the cumulative effect of the proof-of-work helps the network maintain an identical blockchain. The bitcoin software always chooses the longest blockchain as the canonical one. The more blocks, with the most transactions, and the longer hashes from more difficult proof-of-work tasks, will create the longest blockchain. In this way, the network will always select the blockchain with the majority of computers working on it, and ignore any attempt to insert a false blockchain prepared by a minority of attacking machines. There is only ever one, single blockchain, and it will always be the one used by the vast majority of the network.

Once a merchant sees their transaction in a confirmed block in this longest, canonical blockchain, they know that the coins were really transferred. The transaction cannot be cancelled out by a contradicting transaction, and the blockchain will always be the single record of that transaction. Now, a double-spend is nearly impossible.

Trust

Trusting the proof-of-work seems to leave much to chance. What if there are communication disruptions between parts of the network? Trusting the proof-of-work seems to work in theory, but without any authority to say which blockchain is definitely the right one, couldn't there be problems?

Sometimes there is a rare case in which a block is solved by two different computers at different ends of the network, such that each computer thinks it is first because neither has received notification of the other's block yet. Each of those computers, being separated on the network, will log different transactions into its block. In this rare event, the network will have two different ledgers in play for just a moment, a situation called a '**fork**'.

There will be a moment of confusion, as the network receives two different updated blockchains. As soon as the different blocks are solved, each computer in the network will receive either one new block, or the other. The network will be split between the two different ledgers. At some point, however, the next block will be solved, by the half of the network with more computers, and therefore more effort going towards solving the proof-of-work. As this second block is added to one of the two conflicting ledgers, one will suddenly be longer. As the network always selects the longest blockchain, the competing ledger will be discarded in favour of the one already selected by the majority. In essence, on this basis the network votes on which blockchain to use, and then vetoes all others. Before long, the entire network is now on the longest blockchain, and there is only one, canonical ledger again.

Regardless of how close in time the solutions may have been, and however much the transaction records might differ, by the time a second block has been added the network will begin picking one version of the blockchain and stick with it. All the computers will once again agree. This situation is rare, but cautious cryptocurrency users often wait for two or more cycles of confirmed blocks, because then they can be sure that any potential fork was resolved and that the blockchain they are seeing, and the transactions it contains, are the one, true record of every coin and address currency-wide.

Is the blockchain all that it's cracked up to be?

The blockchain, rather than cryptocurrencies, has been lauded as the real invention of note. But many of the ideas involved were invented long before cryptocurrencies came along.

The chain of signatures utilized in a blockchain is called a 'Merkle tree', after its inventor Ralph Merkle, who came up with it in 1979. It is used for all kinds of networked applications that need to share data, ensuring that data isn't corrupted through the chain of shares. Many of these applications are crucial to the functioning of our networked systems.

The blockchain, which is more specifically for multi-user, decentralized ledgers of transaction information, may end up being just as important as the Merkle tree which inspired it. But that all depends on what the blockchain is used for. Many people have big ideas for the blockchain (see Chapter 11), but none of them have truly made their mark yet. Until then, it is just one more clever invention among many others.

5
Mining gold the digital way

How do you generate your own cryptocurrency? What kind of equipment works best? And can lone miners ever really strike it rich?

The world of currency mining

The process of generating cryptocurrency is called 'mining'. But if you imagine this involves pick axes, precious metals or underground tunnels, think again. The only tools you need for this form of mining are a powerful computer, some specialized software and a fast connection to the internet.

As described in the previous chapter, the heart of all proof-of-work cryptocurrencies is a digital ledger called a blockchain. Computers on a cryptocurrency's network continually compete in a race to update this blockchain. It involves a process of brute-force trial and error in which computers simply take guesses at the cryptographic signature, or 'hash', which combines the record of the most recent currency transactions along with the proof-of-work solution and the signature for the previous blocks. When the correct one is found, the new block is added to the blockchain, and the race to find the next hash starts over again.

Suitably equipped, anyone can join this race. But why would you use valuable processing power to take part? This is where the mining analogy arises: the first to solve the block is rewarded with new coins – a gold strike!

The amount of this reward varies between cryptocurrencies, as does the estimated time to solve each block (see box 'What are the rewards?', below). Whether or not this is the best model is still a subject for debate. Other cryptocurrencies have tested different approaches, and all kinds of schemes have been tried. For instance, **litecoin**, created in 2011, experimented by increasing the total number of coins to 84 million, and decreasing the block time to 2½ minutes. **Dogecoin** set its block time to only one minute, and added a wrinkle: it began by awarding a random number of coins for each new block, with the number varying between zero to one million. It has since stabilized this

53

reward. Another cryptocurrency called 42coin was based on the idea that there would never be more than a total of 42 coins in circulation, meaning that hyperdeflation was designed into the algorithm. However 42coin, like many others, is now defunct.

What are the rewards?

In bitcoin's early days, it gave out 50 coins per block, with a target block-calculation time of 10 minutes. After 210,000 blocks had been completed, the reward was automatically cut in half to 25 coins, and after each new 210,000 blocks are solved, the reward is halved again. Eventually, after 6,930,000 blocks have been solved and 21 million bitcoins have been distributed, there will be no more block rewards. It is difficult to predict the time when this will happen, because of slight variances in the time to solve each block. But on July 9, 2016, the third 'halving' occurred, dropping the bitcoin reward down to 12½ per block. This occurred on block number 420,000 – only 6.06% of the way to the final end point. As the decrease of reward reduces exponentially, the reward will slow to a trickle, and then stop. At this point, it is hoped that small transfer fees – of, say, a millionth of a bitcoin deducted from each transaction – will become the block rewards. In other words, this system sets up planned deflation. As the supply of bitcoin approaches the final, fixed amount, each bitcoin will theoretically become more and more valuable so the worth of small transaction fees will rise.

Given the rewards, it might seem that the mining analogy is apt – you invest in equipment and expend energy, utilizing whatever technical advances could give you an edge, all in order to 'discover' or 'mint' an item of value that is often compared to digital gold. Yet this misses the crucial point that if all cryptocurrency mining stopped, every coin in circulation would cease to exist. This form of mining is not discovering or producing any actual object, but instead using cryptography to continuously secure the blockchain via proof-of-work. New coins are merely the programmed reward. It is not a supply chain activity building up the inventory of valuable commodities. It is, in fact, the act of transferring the currency, and the only means by which the currency can even be said to have any use. Mining for cryptocurrency might be better compared to working as a banker, settling accounts and processing transactions in order to support the entire structure of this virtual financial system.

Strength in numbers

The continual race to compute new hash is the lifeblood of any cryptocurrency. The more hash on the network, the better. One way to quantify this is simply in terms of the rate of potential hash solutions produced, expressed as hash per second (h/s). If one computer in the network is producing twice the h/s of another computer, it is doing twice the amount of work to solve the block. Accordingly, that computer would be twice as likely to solve the block and receive its reward. Similarly, if a large number of more powerful computers join a network such that it produces twice the h/s, that network will be expected to find the solution to the block in half the time.

However bitcoin is designed to adjust the difficulty of finding the solution after every 2016 blocks have been completed, in an attempt to establish a nearly constant block time of ten minutes per block. This way, if the **hashrate** of the entire network doubles, the difficulty would then double so that the block still takes the same amount of time to solve. This means transactions continue to be logged to the blockchain at the same rate, and accordingly, new coins flow into the system in a controllable way.

There's another good reason to keep the challenge difficult. The greater the difficulty of the problem to be solved, the harder it will be for anyone to attempt to create a false blockchain and try to pass it off as the real one. Theoretically, a rogue computer could tamper with blocks if it inserted false transactions into the blockchain, and then recalculated all the proof-of-work to catch up with the rest of the network, winning the current block and then presenting its altered blockchain as the actual record. To help prevent this, the network always chooses the longest blockchain, which is the most difficult to solve, in order to make sure any usurper blockchains will struggle to hash all the way back to the end again, and to make sure they must hash as hard or harder than the rest of the network.

Now imagine there are only two computers in the network. An attacker would simply need to have the faster machine to simply outpace the other computer, allowing their false blockchain to be the longest and most difficult to solve. But with hundreds or thousands of computers on a network, the attacking computer would need to be stupendously powerful – not only the fastest, but faster than all the rest working together. Such a theoretical situation is known as a '**51% Attack**', because the attacking computer must be faster than all other computers on the network combined and, hence, create a majority of the hash. So the greater the number of independently controlled computers there are on the network, the more challenging a 51% Attack will be, and the more secure the cryptocurrency.

A digital arms race

Even before it became clear that cryptocurrencies would be worth anything in the real world, it was obvious that those with more powerful computers would be more likely to solve blocks and therefore win more coins. In April 2010, a programmer called Laszlo Hanyecz figured out how to get his computer's graphics processing unit (**GPU**) – a specialized processor board responsible for rendering three-dimensional digital images – to do the hashing for bitcoin rather than his computer's central processing unit (**CPU**). Hashing takes time because it is a very repetitive task, requiring millions of calculations every second. Specialized hardware like a GPU is designed to do large numbers of small tasks very quickly, and so excel at hashing: typically a single GPU can produce a hashrate at least ten times faster than that of a single CPU.

As bitcoin grew more valuable, more computers were connected to the network, and winning rewards became more difficult. Users then began to compete with each other to build powerful 'mining rigs' – towers of computers with multiple GPUs hooked together. This not only increased their personal reward of new bitcoins, but also increased the overall computing power in the network, called the 'global hashrate'. An arms race had begun, with millions of dollars worth of bitcoins at stake for the winners.

Specialized mining equipment

As competition grew, miners began casting around for processors even more powerful than GPUs. The next devices to come under scrutiny were so-called field-programmable gate arrays (**FPGAs**) – logic circuits that could be programmed by their users to accomplish very specific tasks. Meanwhile other devices called application-specific integrated circuits (**ASICs**) were also developed specifically for mining bitcoins. Sold by companies whose sole purpose was to feed the new gold rush, they were essentially bitcoin-mining machines, capable of no other tasks. Plugged into the internet, these devices sent the global hashrate skyrocketing, and quickly made mining no longer cost effective for anyone without such specialized hardware.

Indeed, many bitcoin miners were soon dismayed as their conventional computer hardware became obsolete. Compared to the amount of hash generated by a desktop computer, for example, an ASIC works at a rate more than a million times faster, typically generating gigahash/second (Gh/s) or even terahash/second (Th/s). Clearly, conventional computers were far less likely to earn bitcoins. Meanwhile, those with the most expensive ASICs were raking it in, sometimes earning back their investment of tens of thousands of dollars in equipment in just a few weeks.

In order to counter this escalating arms race, new cryptocurrencies with different hashing algorithms were created. Bitcoin's hashing algorithm is called SHA-256. It is slow, which is thought to make it generally more secure and accurate. Most proof-of-work cryptocurrencies use this algorithm, and the ASICs that were designed to mine bitcoins are only compatible with it. The first alternative algorithm to be introduced was called scrypt – it is the algorithm for the litecoin cryptocurrency. It was designed to run on CPUs, work quicker, and use less electricity. It can be adapted to process blocks in as little as 30 seconds. And for a time, this new algorithm levelled the playing field. But eventually technology caught up, and now there are ASICs that run scrypt as well. There are a few other new algorithms out there too, such as X11 and a proprietary algorithm called Momentum used only for a blockchain service called BitShares. It seems likely that the same hardware arms race which occurred with SHA-256 and scrypt will be repeated with these algorithms too.

Birth of a new industry

As it became harder to make money through cryptocurrency mining, some began to follow the old adage: the way to get rich in a gold rush is to sell shovels. And producing ASIC-based mining equipment – technology good for no purpose other than mining cryptocurrency – soon became an industry in its own right. Unfortunately things got off to a rocky start.

In June 2012, an US company called Butterfly Labs announced that it would be the first company to sell ASICs specifically designed for mining bitcoins, and quickly collected $5 million in pre-orders. However in January 2013, before Butterfly Labs could ship a device, a Chinese company called Avalon pipped it to the post and delivered its own special-ized ASICs to customers. After a flood of complaints about Butterfly Labs, the US Federal Trade Commission shut the company down, though it was later re-opened and began to offer refunds.

This was an omen of things to come. Perhaps encouraged by the opportunity for quick profits, and with sales conducted over the internet, often in non-reversible cryptocurrencies, the coin-mining device industry became a watchword for businesses that, at best, were badly managed and, at worst, downright scams. In March 2014, Fibonacci, a US company based in Florida began to take pre-orders for ASICs to mine scrypt-based crypto-currencies. Within five months, its website had disappeared and the company could no longer be contacted. Estimates in news reports suggest investors lost more than $1 million. The industry has even seen straight-up Ponzi schemes, paying out initial inves-tors using cash from those who invested later, based on early positive reviews. In December 2014, for example, a scrypt-based operation headquartered in Romania called Litecoin GEAR, reportedly stopped making payouts to existing investors when the stream of new investments dried up. Much the same thing allegedly occurred with mining company Bitcoin Trader a few months earlier.

Despite this, it is fair to say that legitimate companies now outweigh the fraudulent, and there are many powerful ASIC machines on the market. Avalon, BitFury, and Bit-Main's AntMiner brand are three highly-regarded offerings, with products that mine at rates from 2 Gh/s to nearly 5 Th/s, depending on configuration and power consumption. Without a doubt these companies are highly profitable, competing with each other to provide the best technology and earn brand recognition.

The emergence of pools

But even with a top-of-the-line ASIC mining a popular currency like bitcoin, any individual miner is still a drop in the ocean. By early summer 2016, solving a block would earn a 25 bitcoin reward, worth over $16,000 on the market, a sum that would more than pay back the cost of the ASIC. However, the global hashrate of bitcoin had reached over 1.5 million Th/s, leaving even the fastest ASIC machine with less than a 1 in 300,000 chance of success. Investing thousands of dollars in cutting edge technology only to earn a chance of earning bitcoins no greater than in the lottery seemed a poor decision. As a cottage industry, it looked like bitcoin mining was dead.

A Chinese bitcoin mine. China is home to the majority of the world's mining pools.

Instead, miners have began to join together to form 'mining pools'. Rather than competing for the tiny chance of winning a whole block reward, they prefer to pool computer power and combine their hash with others. When the pool wins a block the reward is split between members according to their contributed hashrates. This has the effect of averaging out the rewards, turning the profit into a small but steady income. And the larger the pool, the more regular the payout, even if it is just fractions of a coin each day.

Do mining pools have a downside?

It turns out that the rise of pools creates a new risk. Larger pools increase the possibility that one of them may someday acquire 51 per cent of the hashrate, making the blockchain vulnerable to attack. Already, a few heavyweight bitcoin mining pools control the vast majority of the global hashrate. In November 2016, the largest pool was AntPool, the official pool of Chinese ASIC producer Bitmain, with 19 per cent of the hashrate. Close behind was F2Pool, also based in China, with 12.4 per of the hashrate. BTCC Pool had 11.9 per cent, BW had 9.2 per cent and BitFury's official pool had 8.1 per cent. Together, these top five pools control more than 60 per cent of bitcoin mining (see Figure 5.1). Yet there is a clear incentive to prevent any single pool having majority control. Should this occur, it is highly likely that confidence in the cryptocurrency would be eroded, given the technical possibility of that pool altering the block-chain. As these pools rely on bitcoin for profit, any crisis of confidence in the currency would likely destroy their business. As a result, miners often switch between pools, in a concerted attempt to prevent any one pool dominating.

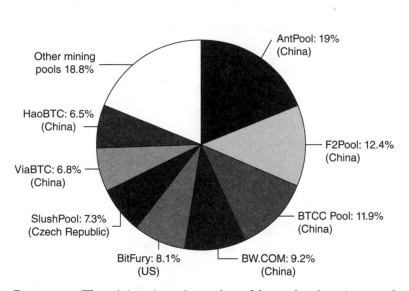

FIGURE 5.1 The mining giants. A snapshot of the market share (measured by hashrate distribution) of the largest mining pools, from November 2016. The distribution is highly variable.

Outsourcing to the cloud

While these large pools now enjoy dominance, another model has emerged which can also offer individuals a way to reap cryptocurrency rewards. Cloud mining works more or less like any other cloud service: a company operates a large centralized facility where it hosts services for paying clients on its own equipment. In the case of bitcoin mining, the customer typically pays the company a rate per hash/s, and is free to purchase as much as they like. Then they gain a percentage of the bitcoins earned.

There are some clear benefits. Rather than investing in your own mining gear, you are investing money in the cloud miner's operation so they can build or buy ASIC units and operate them on an industrial scale. The cloud mining company owns the hardware and facilities, they simply pay out a percentage of profits to their investors who enabled the operation. The company looks after the mining hardware while taking a small percentage of profits to cover operating costs, as well as benefiting from economies of scale. And even if customers depart, the cloud miner still owns the hardware, and can run it themselves for reward. The benefit for the customer is that they need only provide the cash to purchase the hashrate — they don't need to purchase, house or maintain expensive, hot, electricity-guzzling circuitry.

All the hardware itself is housed inside huge warehouses. Although most mining companies are secretive about their operations (not surprising, given the amount of money involved) images posted online that purport to show some of the larger cloud mining companies such as BW.com and Ant-Pool reveal rack upon rack of processors, stacked to the ceiling in vast warehouses, with large cooling fans, thick power cables, and very few humans in sight. To maximize profits, cloud mining services are often based where electricity is cheap — in the vicinity of large hydroelectric generators or geothermal energy sources, for example, or in locations close to the Arctic where cooling the hard-working processors can be as simple as opening a window. For example, cloud mining company Genesis Mining started out with sites in Bosnia and China but is now based in Iceland, thanks to its cheap electricity, cold climate and fast internet links.

No picks and shovels: these energy-hungry processers are mining bitcoins.

A distributed currency with central control

Although cryptocurrency was designed to be distributed across the internet, the realities of the mining process mean it has evolved to become increasingly centralized. A handful of pools now control the vast majority of the global hashrate of bitcoin and these pools distribute much of the new funds generated. It seems that the economic advantage of centralized industry and large-scale production has been enough to drive most of the small mining companies and pools out of business.

Cloud mining is now even looking to court mainstream investors. Genesis Mining has launched the first bitcoin mining fund registered with the U.S. Securities and Exchange Commission, offering investors securities in a mining-based fund called the Logos Fund. As risky and complex as cryptocurrencies can be, there is a growing number of people willing to put down large amounts of money in order to play that risk.

There is another sense in which centralization is a good thing. As the technology in any field develops, new developments can rapidly increase efficiency. Based on a rate of watts-per-hash-generated, an ASIC can be more than 18 million times as efficient in energy consumption as a single CPU. When mining on a vast scale this efficiency means lower electricity bills which could make a huge difference to the bottom line, and makes the bitcoin network less wasteful overall.

How much electricity do miners use?

The energy consumption of mining cryptocurrencies like bitcoin is not small. Extrapolating from one measured rate of energy consumption for the first ASIC-mining machine released in 2013, the global hashrate for bitcoin at that time would have consumed over 482,969 megawatt-hours per year. That is the equivalent of over 44,000 average US homes.

Using figures for ASIC-mining machines released in mid-2016, the electricity consumption for bitcoin seems to have increased substantially to 3.36 million megawatt-hours per year, or the equivalent of over 307,000 average US homes. Note, however, that this is a power increase of only 7 times, despite a global hashrate some 184 times higher than in 2013. A mining pool utilizing ASICs may put small-scale miners out of business, but it certainly helps save large amounts of electricity in the process.

Size really does matter

But scale does bring its own problems. The larger the pool, the more it tends to draw hacking attacks. One study shows that 63 per cent of large bitcoin pools have come under attack from hackers, while only 17 per cent of smaller pools have been targeted. By staying under the radar, small pools may be avoiding some of the troubles experienced by larger pools.

There is also some concern in the mining community over the extent to which having mining centralized in large pools could create problems for the future of a cryptocurrency. The collective of individuals working to update the code for bitcoin are attempting to solve certain problems with regard to how well the currency scales to more users (see 'Nakamoto's successors work on revamping the bitcoin', Chapter 11). But for a software update to be accepted, everyone in the network has to agree to the update. This serves as a form of voting: when a majority of the network has updated to a new version, it is considered to be accepted, and the old version is phased out. However, if the new version is not accepted, developers have to go back to the drawing board.

Currently, the pools that control the majority of the bitcoin network have been sceptical of recently proposed software changes, and have turned them down. Cultural differences between different pools may also be playing a role here – many pools are in China, for example, while most of the software developers are in the US. And there is some concern that if a conservative instinct takes hold and updates are resisted, in the long term the currency might stagnate.

Of course bitcoin is only one cryptocurrency among many, although it is the biggest in value and in network size. Miners will often switch the currency they mine on a daily or hourly basis. And while it is unlikely that bitcoin will fall from the top of the heap, new blockchains are always being introduced. In 2016, for example, two new sorts of blockchains, **Ethereum** and **Ripple**, have emerged and surpassed a horde of other cryptocurrencies to become the second and third largest by market capital behind bitcoin. As the economic and technological conditions governing the mining process continue to evolve, so too will the status quo.

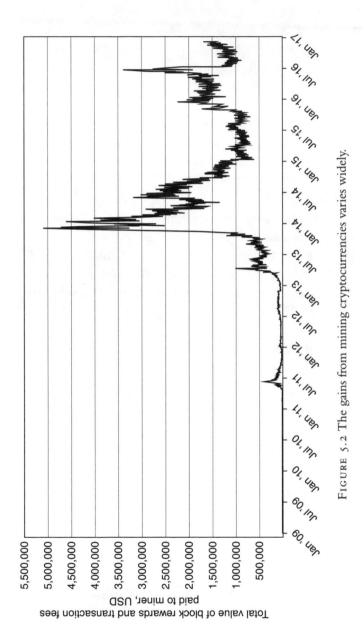

FIGURE 5.2 The gains from mining cryptocurrencies varies widely.

6
Assassins and drugs: Spending bitcoin in the early days

From their inception, cryptocurrencies have been associated with the criminal underbelly of the internet. This is epitomized by tale of Silk Road, the first cryptocurrency marketplace, and the downfall of its founder, Dread Pirate Roberts.

The news stories sound like the plot points of a conspiracy thriller. Murder for hire. Drug trafficking. Embezzlement. Fraud. Money laundering. Corruption. Market manipulation. The environment at risk. Governments on track to be overthrown. 'Bitcoin is evil', says a Nobel Prize-winning economist in the pages of the *New York Times*. 'Malware turns hacked computers into slaves that 'mine' new digital currency', reports tech publication *Quartz*. One of CNN's many headlines on bitcoin read, 'Bitconned: SEC busts alleged bitcoin Ponzi scheme'. *Forbes* magazine reported, 'FBI says it's seized $28.5 million in bitcoins'.

Are cryptocurrencies the latest tool of cybervillians? Are they digital bombs, thrown into the new electronic economy? It might seem so from the coverage of cryptocurrencies in the media. By the time media articles about bitcoin exploded in early 2011 with the opening of Silk Road, it was clear that the cryptocurrency would be valuable. But no one was sure who would be making the money: scammers, drug dealers, or legitimate investors. Two years later, with a list of individuals facing lengthy prison sentences, it wasn't clear who had won the race – only who had lost.

Silk Road

By far the largest flirtation between bitcoin and criminality was Silk Road. In this story, we see the ideal of an anonymous, non-governmental currency pushed to its breaking point. We see how a seemingly normal second-hand book salesman picked up a life sentence in federal prison. He became the centre of a huge FBI dragnet; the target of a massive operation spanning numerous US federal law enforcement agencies. None of this would ever have happened without bitcoin.

Timeline: The path of Silk Road

- **January 2011** Ross Ulbricht develops Silk Road, a market-place for illicit substances, and begins quietly advertising it on bitcoin and drug forums. Bitcoin is trading around 30 cents.
- **June 2011** Gawker publishes a story about Silk Road. Price of bitcoin hits new high of $30.
- **August 2011** Silk Road generates $30,000 worth of commissions in one month.
- **December 2011** FBI and other law enforcement agencies purchase more than 100 shipments of drugs from the site, gathering information and making arrests.
- **March 2012** Silk Road generates $90,000 worth of commissions in one month.
- **November 2012** Silk Road begins paying protection money to hackers who threaten to shut down the site with a distributed denial-of-service (DDoS) attack.
- **January 2013** After site administrator Curtis Green is arrested in a sting operation, Ross Ulbricht allegedly attempts to have him killed, unaware that he is hiring an undercover DEA agent to do so.
- **July 2013** Ulbricht's own personal account receives nearly $20,000 per day in Silk Road commissions. Law enforcement learns this as they close in on Silk Road servers in Iceland.
- **October 2013** After connecting an email account owned by Ulbricht to internet posts involving Silk Road, agents arrest him at a San Francisco public library. They seize his computer, which is logged in to Silk Road administrator accounts.
- **May 2015** After a trial in which he claims he was framed, Ulbricht is convicted and sentenced to life in prison.

The beginning of dealing drugs digitally

In January 2011, a post appeared on a 'magic mushroom' website called shroomery.org. Written by a user named 'altoid', it posted a link to a site called Silk Road and asked if anyone had any experience using it. Days later, a user by the same name posted on bitcointalk.org, with a similar message.

Two years later, in 2013, FBI agents would discover that these two posts were the earliest references to Silk Road on the internet – meaning they were likely to have been written by the site's creator. At this point, the FBI didn't have a name for the Silk Road's founder, but the posts would end up being some of the first footprints that investigators found leading to Ross Ulbricht.

Despite the many steps that Ulbricht had taken to keep his identity secret, extraordinary government resources were put into exposing him. He wanted to be an anonymous, online, libertarian hero, and often used the alias 'Dread Pirate Roberts' (DPR), in homage to the character in *The Princess Bride,* to keep his name away from Silk Road. But in the end, a series of simple missteps lead to his unmasking and arrest.

A strong tool in DPR's arsenal was the web-traffic anonymizing software Tor, which is used by hackers and spies alike to hide their traffic online. By operating Silk Road as a 'hidden service' on the dark web, there was no way that investigators could find the servers hosting the site and shut them down. By using Tor connections for email, chat, and all connections to the administration tasks of Silk Road, DPR and its administrators would remain faceless, nameless, and location-less – as they believed the internet was meant to be. And bitcoin was the cryptocurrency that provided the motivation for their efforts.

Bitcoin wasn't perfectly anonymous, but it could not be shut down by the government, and user accounts could not be closed, unlike credit cards or online merchant services like Paypal. Tor enabled Silk Road to set up its market, and bitcoin allowed for the payment of the goods. It seemed like the whole enterprise was risk free.

Was Silk Road ever really anonymous?

The Silk Road marketplace was supposed to be completely anonymous. But while Tor worked well to disguise the source and destination of internet traffic, bitcoin transactions could be traced through the blockchain, meaning they were never entirely secret.

The site's technology was not perfect, either. Ulbricht caught a number of early security flaws in the site with the help of volunteers. The fact that people had come forward after spotting the vulnerabilities reinforced Ulbricht's belief that the site could survive with self-policing. In his idealistic view, he thought that the site's users and the technology were more powerful than the forces out to get them, and that they would protect each other. But it was one of these security flaws, introduced through a coding error that allowed police to discover the location of the servers in 2013 and gather the evidence that would lead to Ulbricht's conviction.

Except, of course, for the problem that drugs are physical things and had to be delivered in person. This meant that Silk Road sellers had to use the mail and ended up giving the authorities the first real tip-off that there was a new game in town. After an increase in detected drug shipments was noticed, it was only a matter of time between somebody got caught.

Among the many sting operations conducted to intercept mail shipments, the DEA netted one of the secondary administrators of Silk Road in 2013, a user going by the name chronicpain. DEA agents used his administrative accounts to seize $350,000 worth of bitcoins.

When DPR saw that the funds were gone and read in the news that chronicpain (real name Curtis Green) had been arrested, he took a big step towards becoming a real drugs kingpin – he allegedly decided to have Green killed. His assassin would be an acquaintance that he had met through Silk Road. 'Nob' claimed to work with drugs cartels, and often bragged about his violent exploits, so it seemed that he would be an excellent choice. However, Nob was actually a DEA agent called Carl Force IV – the same agent who had just arrested Green. Force staged the execution of Green, engineering what appeared to DPR to be the end of the matter.

Was there an ideology behind Silk Road?

Ross Ulbricht began Silk Road not only for the money but also for the idea. His dream was a digital marketplace, hidden by encryption, in which anyone could conduct any business transaction that they liked, free from the prying eyes of government.

This is an ideal shared by many early proponents of cryptocurrencies, including Satoshi Nakamoto who focused on the currency's ability to function without a banking institution involved, and therefore, as an alternative to traditional 'fiat' currencies such as dollars and euros.

In Nakamoto's internet forum posts, he invoked the unfolding bank crisis as a partial justification for the cryptocurrency. Without any central bank, without any corporate entities, the only thing that bitcoin required anyone to trust is the code that constituted it, open-source and available for review. Other cypherpunks were interested in the notion of privacy. Without needing any ID or licence to hold or trade cryptocurrency, they felt that they could conduct transactions without anyone prying into their business. And naturally, it wasn't just their neighbours they were concerned about, but governments and tax authorities.

CAPTCHA leads to capture

In June 2013, a separate FBI investigation team uncovered a piece of information from the Silk Road site that ought to have been hidden. One of the tools used to keep bots from flooding Silk Road with faulty logins, called **CAPTCHA**, had leaked the **IP address** of where the Silk Road servers were located: Iceland. DPR and his associates were nowhere nearby. Connecting only through the encrypted layers of Tor, the users, the administrators, and the servers were all isolated from each other across the internet. But after the CAPTCHA leak the FBI had found the servers' location. Armed with diplomatic letters, they went to Iceland to get a copy of the server. This provided them with a key source of evidence that would be used to find and eventually convict DPR.

After investigating the server, the FBI found that a series of connections had been made without using Tor, but instead using VPN services. These Virtual Private Networks (VPN) also allow people to mask their internet traffic, but only by relaying it through another computer. By tracing back the logins, investigators were able to see that many of the connections had come from locations in the San Francisco area.

Meanwhile, an IRS agent working with the team found a post on a programming website asking for help setting up Tor hidden services, using the same username 'altoid' from the posts on shroomery.org and bitcointalk.org in 2011. An email address, 'rossulbricht@gmail.com', was connected to that username. For the FBI, the pieces were starting to fall into place and a picture began to emerge.

After finding a number of other synchronicities, including a Homeland Security report about fake IDs being shipped to Ulbricht's house, the FBI began surveillance. They watched as Ulbricht logged on to his computer, and DPR suddenly appeared on Silk Road. This happened time after time. Soon, they had enough evidence for a warrant and in a surprise sting, they cornered Ulbricht in a San Francisco public library, managing to seize his computer intact as he was logged in to the administrator accounts of Silk Road.

Not everyone was happy to see Ross Ulbricht, the Silk Road creator, on trial.

In May 2015, Ulbricht was sentenced to life in prison without parole. It seems the jury was persuaded by the overwhelming evidence seized by the FBI, complete with chat logs that served as a day-by-day history of his orchestration of the massive scheme. However, murder-for-hire was dropped from the indictment. It seems that the supposed murder of Curtis Green, as well as a number of murders which Ulbricht thought he was paying for, never happened. Some were schemes orchestrated by police; others were scams to deprive DPR of bitcoin.

Astonishingly, Carl Force IV, the DEA agent who set up the sting and simulated murder of Curtis Green, was himself arrested for pocketing bitcoin seized from Silk Road, as well as abusing legal authority in several other ways to hide his theft of the money. A Secret Service agent was also prosecuted along with him and they are both now serving time in prison. Ross Ulbricht's attorney is planning an appeal based on the episode. (There is also an indictment in the US District Court of Maryland, which includes murder-for-hire charges, that is still pending.) It seems that the size of the fortune contained within Silk Road corrupted the authorities, as much as the perpetrator.

Life after Silk Road

Silk Road was finished, but lingering questions and loose ends still remain. In late 2015, another of the original Silk Road administrators going by the name Variety Jones was arrested in Thailand. This came three months after he had posted a bizarre story on an online forum alleging that he was being hunted and threatened by a corrupt FBI agent, who wanted his help to access $70 million in bitcoins not yet seized by authorities, perhaps by torturing Ross Ulbricht's family. This story might sound absurd, except for the fact that two federal agents had already been prosecuted for stealing illicit cryptocurrency from Silk Road. No outside confirmation of Jones' story has yet appeared.

Meanwhile, although the criminal complaint against Ulbricht listed the information gleaned from the CAPTCHA leak and the 'altoid' online postings as the evidence that led the FBI to identify DPR, it has since become apparent that the Tor network was compromised at least once. In 2014, researchers from Carnegie Mellon University, along with the Department of Defense, were able to compromise enough Tor nodes to expose the IP address of a Brian Farrell. This information was then used by the FBI to prosecute Farrell for his involvement in running one of the Silk Road's successor websites. Although the Tor Project has now claimed to have fixed this particular vulnerability, there have been speculations that perhaps this exploit was also used in the investigation of the original Silk Road.

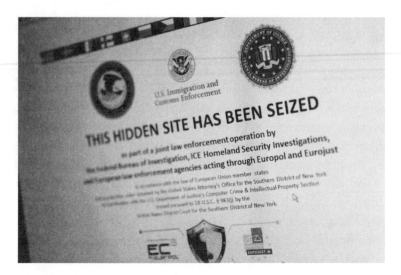

Silk Road and many copycat sites were shut down by the US authorities.

Selling drugs online using bitcoin, while not a foolproof scheme, still seems to be too great a money maker for others not to try their hand. Several Silk Road copycats have sprung up in its wake. Some have been shut down by authorities, others were apparently scams, and yet others persist to this day, selling drugs and other illegal services online, so far dodging the police that hunt them through the dark webs of the internet.

Where next?

Throughout the brief history of cryptocurrencies and blockchain technologies, the media has been captivated with the fact that these tools were invented in the dark hacker realms of the internet. But, cryptocurrencies aren't, themselves, illegal. In fact, the amount of crime conducted via cryptocurrencies pales in comparison to the amount of crime occurring in the markets of regular, old-fashioned currency.

In between the headlines lies the true story. The idealistic dream of evolving money and business transactions to ensure a new level of technologically-secured personal privacy had been realized, but soon met the harsh realities of greed and governance as the value of cryptocurrencies grew to billions of dollars and inherited some of the issues of traditional currencies. Programmers and government regulators are still trying to unravel the technical and legal complications around cryptocurrencies today. But within all of those complications was the kernel of a new idea. And that new idea, no matter how complex, political, dangerous, or flawed, is not going away. Through this trial by fire, cryptocurrency emerged, perhaps even stronger than ever, with new investors ready to play by the rules (see 'Bitcoin by post' and 'Bitcoin accountants', Chapter 8).

The legend of Dread Pirate Roberts

So brazen were the attempts of Ross Ulbricht (aka Dread Pirate Roberts) to thwart the law, that they can make him seem like an most legendary character. Some regarded him as a modern-day Robin Hood. In his many written missives on Silk Road, DPR certainly promoted this legend among his fans and supporters. This put him in contrast to the anonymous creator of bitcoin, who vanished rather than become a caricature of mystique that might damage his creation.

The users of Silk Road bought into the mystique. Users compared DPR to Che Guevara, praised him for creating jobs, and even joined the Silk Road book club, to discuss books on politics, economics, law, and other topics. All with a libertarian bent, of course.

Silk Road acted like a floating pirate ship on the high seas of the internet. The administrators of Silk Road were the only arbiters of what was allowed for sale. Silk Road policy was clear – only 'victimless' items could be traded. This meant the site centred primarily on drugs and forged IDs. Illegal pornography, weapons, or stolen goods were forbidden. To ensure everyone got the standard of product that they were hoping for, users themselves rated their transactions in a 'trust' system, not unlike eBay or other commerce sites. The system was intended to identify scammers, and prevent undercover police from posing as sellers or customers.

But the vetting process for customers and sellers wasn't as effective as hoped. By November of 2011, police had made over 100 undercover purchases from Silk Road, leading to a number of arrests. This netted them at least two Silk Road administrators who turned over their accounts to the police, which were then used by officers to fully infiltrate the site.

With the benefit of hindsight, it seems that Ross Ulbricht was not quite as swashbuckling as he was idealistic and naive. Ulbricht was no hardened criminal, at least at the outset. His initial crime was to grow a small crop of magic mushrooms and figure out a way to sell them online. But this ultimately led to his downfall.

7
The school of hard Gox

With millions of dollars worth of commissions every month, the cryptocurrency exchange Mt. Gox was surely too big to fail. Or was it?

The bitcoin exchange

Technology flaws were rampant in the early days of the crypto-currency world. While the coding of bitcoin itself was proving to be resilient, the infrastructure required to buy and sell bitcoins in a currency exchange was not quite as secure, leaving it open to attack by hackers.

Mt. Gox, the primary web exchange for bitcoin at the time that Silk Road launched in 2011, was first hit by hackers back when its creator, Jed McCaleb, was still in control. The theft was minimal, but this attack raised McCaleb's awareness of how vulnerable the site was. The episode was a major influence in his decision to sell Mt. Gox to **Mark Karpeles**, a programmer he had befriended who was helping manage the site. The sale took place in March 2011, but the problems with hackers didn't stop there. In June 2011, there was another break-in.

Somehow, a hacker had managed to forge the credentials needed to log into Jed McCaleb's still-active account with full administrator privileges. This gave the intruder the ability to artificially boost their account holdings, creating 100,000 bitcoins where none existed before. They couldn't fool the bitcoin blockchain, but they didn't need to. The fake bitcoins only existed in the internal accounting of the Mt. Gox website. When users traded currency on Mt. Gox, they transferred bitcoins to the Mt. Gox public address, which tracked their balances internally as they bought and sold. The exchange then sent bitcoins out of the Mt. Gox wallet back to the users when they wished to withdraw their funds. With a new fortune existing only inside the Mt. Gox system, the hacker began selling rapidly, sending the price of bitcoin on the exchange plummeting. Within 30 minutes, the price had crashed from $17.50 to $0.01.

Mt. Gox had a security measure: only $1,000 worth of bitcoins could be transferred out of the site's wallet, via the blockchain, at a time. But with the price artificially low, this was a lot more coins than before. The attacker withdrew funds, transferring 2,000 bitcoins out of Mt. Gox – real bitcoins from Mt. Gox's coffers, not just figments of the Mt. Gox account software. As the price rebounded after the sell-off, those bitcoins became worth far more than $1,000. A month later, that sum could have been worth $13,000.

The result of the attack was chaos. The price had crashed and rebounded, and hundreds of Mt. Gox users, thinking they were getting a bargain, had exchanged real dollars for the fake bitcoins. Mt. Gox had to shut down to audit its exchange accounts and remove the fake bitcoins. This left the users in a panic, unsure if their accounts were still active, were drained of funds, or had succumbed to some other form of sabotage. Furthermore, the hacker posted data stolen during the intrusion to the internet, which added to the confusion.

Eventually, Mt. Gox sorted everything out, erased the trading history that occurred after the engineered crash, and repaid the missing bitcoins from its own pockets. But it was a blow both to the exchange and to the cryptocurrency, in general. Even though bitcoin had only ever functioned exactly as it was supposed to, if the biggest bitcoin exchange was vulnerable to price manipulation and theft, what did this mean for its future?

The fall of the exchange

Despite hacker attacks and near-constant technical problems, Mark Karpeles kept trying to make Mt. Gox work. By March 2013 he had 18 people working for him, including someone to lead the business while he handled the site's functionality. Karpeles was the only person who could approve of changes to the code, including major security fixes.

Mt. Gox was earning trading commissions of over one million dollars per month, but slip-ups persisted. A deal with startup CoinLab to handle US bank transactions ended in a lawsuit in May 2013 because of Mt. Gox's failure to uphold its end of the bargain – the contract was supposed to give CoinLab exclusive access to Mt. Gox accounts in North America, but the company was still using other deposit processors. Later that month, the US Department of Homeland Security seized Mt. Gox accounts managed by payment processor, Dwolla, because the exchange had not registered as a money transmitting company, even though other bitcoin businesses had done so with ease.

In February 2014, the deathblow for Mt. Gox finally landed. It began, as many of Mt. Gox's problems did, with a hacker. But this time, it was not a hit-and-run heist. The hacker had been working inside the site for months, maybe even years. Using a known vulnerability in the bitcoin blockchain called the 'transaction malleability problem', the hacker sent coins out from the Mt. Gox wallet, and then made it appear to Mt. Gox as if it the transaction was cancelled (see box 'The transaction malleability problem', below).

Other exchanges had dealt with this vulnerability easily, making their software wait for several block confirmations to reveal whether the bitcoins had been moved, rather than relying on the transaction ID alone. Mt. Gox did not.

The transaction malleability problem

When a bitcoin transaction is sent to the blockchain, it includes a transaction ID number that is created from a cryptographic hash of the sender's address and other transaction information – essentially a unique string of characters, derived from the address and other transaction

---

information. This is a different 'hash' than the hash that is generated by cryptocurrency mining, and different again from the hash of preceding blocks that link the blockchain, but it is a similar cryptographic process. The transaction ID hash is a crucial part of the procedure of signing and verifying the transactions.

After sending a transaction to the blockchain, the bitcoin software on a particular computer will look for the transaction ID number to make sure its transaction was accepted and included in the blockchain. However, a slight flaw in the bitcoin protocol allowed the transaction to still go through if the address was improperly formatted. This slight change in address information would change the cryptographic hash, and accordingly, change the transaction ID number. The computer would look for what it supposed the transaction ID to be, but would not find it. And yet, the transaction would still have gone through.

So, as the hacker created transfer requests out of Mt. Gox, they simultaneously caused Mt. Gox to send the network additional transactions requesting the same transfer of bitcoins, but with an improperly formatted address, and therefore different transaction ID numbers. Doing this continuously, some of the mutated transactions were received and authenticated by the blockchain before the properly formatted ones. Then when Mt. Gox's properly formatted transactions arrived in the network, they were ignored as duplicates.

When the Mt. Gox software looked for its transaction on the blockchain, it would not find the transaction IDs it was looking for, because it was only looking for the properly formatted ones. But the bitcoins would already have been transferred to the hacker's address, using the mutated transactions. So the Mt. Gox software would send more. By continuing this cycle over and over, the hacker got Mt. Gox to transfer twice as many bitcoins as it intended. This is not quite the same as the double-spend problem, but revealed an odd vulnerability that was not initially envisioned by Satoshi Nakamoto and the other early bitcoin coders. It was called the 'transaction malleability problem'.

Most services have learned how to secure themselves against this problem. Rather than looking for the transaction ID specifically, they check to see if the transaction of bitcoin itself is in the blockchain, bypassing the problem of mutated IDs. But the transaction malleability problem continues to crop up in certain bitcoin-using software to this day, and a full fix has yet to be implemented (see 'A possible fix: Segregated witness', Chapter 11).

Over a long period, the hacker slowly made hidden transfers out of the Mt. Gox active, or 'hot', wallet while the website acted as if nothing out of the ordinary had happened. When the wallet was empty, Karpeles unwittingly refilled it with bitcoins from other backup wallets. Like a slow leak, funds trickled out of the Mt. Gox supply, while the site's own internal accounting showed that there were just as many as there ought to have been. The problem wasn't discovered until almost all of Mt. Gox's coins in its many wallets were gone: 100,000 of its own, and 750,000 of its customers'. At the February 2014 price of around $539 per bitcoin, the loss was equivalent to more than $450 million dollars. On 7 February 2014, Mt. Gox froze all account withdrawals. On 24 February, all trading was suspended. The exchange was now closed, forever.

Many people lost money with the fall of Mt. Gox.

Scammers and malware

As well as the high-profile troubles that faced bitcoin, involving the FBI and other federal investigators, there were a slew of minor scams and hacks. Perhaps the very first cryptocurrency Ponzi scheme occurred in 2011, known by the name of Bitcoin Savings & Trust. Like many such scams, it promised returns on investment just too good to be true. After taking in 500,000 bitcoins, the site disappeared in 2012. A group of hackers and others from the bitcoin community discovered the operator's true name and location later that year. That man, Trendon Shavers, was arrested in 2013, and pleaded guilty to securities fraud in 2015.

Also in 2011, reports of bitcoin-specific **malware** first appeared. A program called a 'trojan' (after the mythical Trojan Horse) was discovered in June 2011, that searched users' computers for their secret bitcoin wallet.dat file. After copying and sending the file to the malware authors, they would be able to steal all the bitcoins that user held. That same year, it was reported that a botnet – a large network of compromised computers under the control of hackers – was being put to work mining bitcoins. While the CPUs of the seized computers were not very efficient on their own, if they numbered in the thousands and were connected like a mining pool, it could be quite profitable. Increases in difficulty and the rise of ASICs for mining has made this potential exploit much less likely today.

However, in March 2014, Mt. Gox announced that it had 'found' 200,000 bitcoins in an old wallet. It was an embarrassing, if welcome admission, but it also made many suspicious. Later that month, two Swiss researchers, Christian Decker and Roger Wattenhofer, who had been studying the transaction malleability problem before the announcement of the Mt. Gox fiasco, came forward to say that they had data to show that there was no way that Mt. Gox could have lost as much as they claimed via the flaw. They claimed that, before Mt. Gox froze all account withdrawals in early February, only 386 bitcoins had ever been stolen using malleability attacks.

Debate still continues about what really happened at Mt. Gox, but regardless of the real reason for the loss, there was no way that Mt. Gox could refund their customers' funds. On 28 February 2014, Mt. Gox filed for bankruptcy in Japan, and on 10 March the company filed for bankruptcy in the US. In April 2014, the US Department of Treasury issued a subpoena to Karpeles to question him about the bankruptcy case, for which he declined to appear. On 11 September 2015, the Japanese government arrested him in Japan, charging him with embezzlement in the wake of the bankruptcy.

An interesting coda to the story is that in May 2016, a different exchange called Kraken, which was helping with the bankruptcy analysis of Mt. Gox, reported that it would be releasing the approximately 200,000 'found' bitcoins back to the former customers of the closed exchange, based on their resolution of more than 24,000 claims submitted. No further information was released about their investigations. It appears that the ignominious saga of Mt. Gox is ongoing.

Other cryptocurrency exchanges were also hit by hackers, who broke into computer systems to steal backup files, or simply called up an exchange's hosting company pretending to be the owner and demanding that the administrator password be reset. Other online wallet companies simply vanished, taking their customers' bitcoins with them. It is also important to put the problems that beset Mt. Gox in a wider context of the internet itself. Internet security is a tough business. An estimated $80 billion is now spent on cybersecurity every year. Despite this, around 64 million Americans had their personal data breached just *in the last year*, according to a 2016 RAND Corporation report.

Encryption kidnappers

Another problem to beset cryptocurrency is **ransomware** – malicious software that blocks access to a computer system until a sum of money is paid. Although ransomware attacks were first seen in 1989, in 2013 a new generation of ransomware became widespread, utilizing public-key encryption and bitcoin. The first such program, called CryptoLocker, would encrypt the entire infected computer's data, and then present a pop-up window with a ransom message. The computer user would be told to send a specific amount of bitcoin to a particular address by a deadline. The amount of bitcoin was relatively low, typically around $400-worth. If the ransom was paid, the user would be given a key to decrypt their data. If not, it would remain encrypted forever. Authorities shut down CryptoLocker's controlling botnet in June 2014, but it is estimated that the ransomware netted as much as $27 million. A wave of copycat ransomwares followed. The attacks became so widespread, that certain versions had online help websites, providing information for the uninitiated on how to buy bitcoins to pay their ransoms, and how to decrypt their files once they had paid. 2016 proved to be a banner year for ransomware, netting more than $209 million in the first three months alone, according to an FBI report.

Perhaps a key reason for the increase is that ransomware designers are searching out specific targets with larger budgets. CryptoLocker spread at random, and the low ransom was clearly designed for everyday home and office computers. However, 2016 has seen a number of hospitals targeted directly by customized ransomware, designed to hold medical records and crucial prescription information hostage. Hollywood Hospital in California was targeted by ransomware in February 2016, and hospital officials reportedly paid $17,000 to get crucial records decrypted.

The story of Mt. Gox gave cryptocurrencies bad press, and could have been their undoing. Instead, other exchanges picked up after Mt. Gox closed down. Relative to the market commotions of late 2013 and 2014, when the price of a bitcoin oscillated between a low of $150 and a high of $1200, 2015 was a calm year in trading, with steady volume and prices between $200 and $300. 2016 has seen a new increase in prices, topping over $600 by July (see Figure 1.2, Chapter 1).

Perhaps the greatest testament to cryptocurrencies' longevity is that they managed to weather this storm, and come out the other side with businesses, consumers, and the government still interested in what cryptocurrencies hold for the future.

8
Bitcoin comes of age

From underground beginnings, the world's most famous cryptocurrency is going mainstream. Bitcoin banking is here, and cryptocurrency technology is being included in the longer term strategies of financial institutions and governments. So why is its use in daily life still limited?

Cryptocurrency technology is becoming part of the medium-term strategy of global financial institutions, including banks, investment houses, and even the economic plans of national governments. Investors are putting money directly into crypto-currencies, as well as attempting to leverage them in new types of cryptocurrency-linked services offered by otherwise traditional companies and banks. Despite the false starts represented by Silk Road and Mt. Gox, there are many people who believe that these technologies could fundamentally change the way we use money – and do it legally.

But cryptocurrencies themselves are only the beginning of a brave new world of digital financial technologies. The blockchain is moving away from being simply the technological backbone for a currency, and beginning to support the mechanisms of banks themselves, including property transactions, various electronic transfer services, and, maybe one day, entire corporations.

Bitcoin ATMs are still a rare sight.

Today, the ground-floor of a completely new sort of financial technology is being built. Your first encounter with a cryptocurrency might be in the lobby of your local bank, across the counter of a neighbourhood coffee shop, in the back of a cab, or within the digital deeds of your new house. And you might not even notice.

What can you buy?

One of the most common criticisms of cryptocurrencies is that they will never replace traditional currencies because they are useless as an everyday means of payment (see box 'A day of bitcoin', below). This was certainly true back in the days when the most common market for cryptocurrencies was an illegal drugs website on the dark web. But what about today? The use of cryptocurrency has expanded into the realm of legitimate business, but is it enough to allow cryptocurrency to replace the daily use of pounds, dollars, euros, and yuan?

When companies first began experimenting with accepting cryptocurrencies for products and services, they largely had to invent their own integration with the cryptocurrency on the fly. Today, many companies are offering different forms of cryptocurrency integration as a service, expanding the options and offering easy access for companies. However, there are many different ways to go about integrating cryptocurrency with a business, and no standard method has yet emerged. Confusion continues about what the best way to use cryptocurrency is, from the standpoint of both businesses and consumers.

A day of bitcoin

In February 2014, New Scientist reporter Hal Hodson attempted to use no money other than bitcoin. What did he find?

A third-degree Facebook friend, Michael Giovinco, agrees to sell me $150 of bitcoins to make the journey to New York. I tell him that I plan to use it to drive there, stop at a New Jersey bathhouse on the way, and then head into the city to buy some groceries to stock up my girlfriend's apartment. Giovinco, who has held about 600 bitcoins since 2012, chuckles. 'How do you plan to do that?'

One way to spend cryptocurrency.

Ah, I see. Fuel is the biggest hitch in a bitcoin roadtrip. Only two gas stations in the US accept it – one in Colorado and one in New Hampshire. Neither is on my route. Instead, I try an elaborate workaround involving electronic gift cards and Walmart. It fails. If I'd planned the trip further in advance, I could have bought a preloaded gas card using bitcoins through a website called Coinfueled. Never mind.

Halfway through my journey, I at least find fuel for myself. I fill up on a large burger and fries at TGI Friday's, paid for with a gift card bought with bitcoins via a third-party site.

Deep in the suburbs of New Jersey, just around the corner from a tax office, is a Russian bathhouse – a *banya*. Bear and Birch is run by ex-Goldman Sachs equities trader Peter Kizenko. Inside, you don a bathing suit and join a handful of gruff Russians to brave the searing heat. There's a bundle of birch twigs with a duct-taped handle that you can soak in icy water and thrash yourself with. All for just 0.03 bitcoins.

'It's the easiest thing ever to start accepting it,' says Kizenko, reclining on the veranda of the bathhouse. He started the bathhouse two years ago, after leaving his job with Goldman Sachs in Moscow and finding he missed his homeland's banya. The IRS office might be just around the corner but it is still unclear how bitcoin should be taxed. Kizenko isn't worried, not least because it is too small a part of his revenue and he says the public blockchain, which records every transaction, will make compliance a doddle.

But while accepting the currency is easy, doing anything else with it, like converting it into dollars, is less so, Kizenko says. Several exchanges have been shut down by the authorities recently, making it too risky to base a business on it.

After the bathhouse, I head for Brooklyn's Greene Ave Market. It's a 24-hour organic grocery store offering 10 per cent off for those paying with bitcoins, one of just a handful of places in New York that accepts the currency for physical goods.

Ali, the shop assistant, whips out a cell phone and texts me the string of numbers and letters that serves as the shop's bitcoin address. After I transfer 0.07 bitcoins, he calls his boss to check the payment came through. Other customers catch my eye, disconcerted by this odd transaction. It was simpler at Bear and Birch, where I just scanned a barcode.

For now, there are surprisingly few outlets that accept bitcoin in NYC, considering the attention it has had in the past year. A dog-walking business called Puppy Paws in Brooklyn takes it, as does a pizza joint closer to the river called Lean Crust and a bar called EVR. A handful of legal offices, dentists and estate agents accept it. Throughout my trip, though, the question 'Do you take bitcoin?' is generally met with puzzled looks.

Later, I head to the new bitcoin center in the heart of Wall Street, sandwiched between the towers of traditional finance. Aficionados run their own bitcoin trading floor, named Satoshi Square after the currency's mysterious creator. On the evening that I visit, the topic for discussion is Ethereum, a new platform for virtual currencies.

Those on the cutting edge need no convincing – for them, the revolution is here. But when you can't do much more than buy pizza in New York City, you know bitcoin still has a long way to go.

From dollars to bitcoin via Japan

In the early days of bitcoin, one of the most readily apparent business models enabled by the cryptocurrency was the exchange. Before Mt. Gox, the only way to acquire bitcoins, other than mining them, was by purchasing them from another user on an ad hoc basis. Mt. Gox created the first currency exchange,

THE END OF MONEY

allowing users to buy bitcoins in a market for yen or dollars. From the small commission that Mt. Gox charged, the service was at times earning as much as $900,000 in a single day.

However, Mt. Gox had its weaknesses. In order to get dollars into the Mt. Gox system, it was necessary to wire money to the exchange's Japanese bank – no small feat for the average consumer.

Other exchanges and startups attempted to make this easier. BitInstant, founded in 2011 by US entrepreneurs Gareth Nelson and Charlie Shrem, was one of the first services to allow customers to buy bitcoins on a much more 'retail' basis. The company would handle all of the wire transfers with Mt. Gox, and the customers were simply charged the money and sent the bitcoins. However, first the popular service became so slow that a class action lawsuit was filed in 2013. Then, to seal the company's fate, Shrem was arrested in 2014 and charged with money laundering, for his part in a scheme to sell bitcoins to users of Silk Road. BitInstant shutdown.

How stable are cryptocurrencies?

There are a number of criticisms of cryptocurrencies. Although there are cryptocurrency exchanges, without any of the traditional hedges of conventional asset or exchange markets, the prices of the currencies on these exchanges are vulnerable to manipulation and wild swings. Typically, conventional asset markets have ways to 'bet against' a price increase or insure against a price drop. This also helps equalize market forces that would otherwise create investment bubbles. Although these sorts of derivative assets do exist for cryptocurrency markets, they are nowhere near as widely used as in traditional markets, and thus their ability to help support market stability is unknown.

In the world of finance, size seems to matter. While the markets for cryptocurrencies are large, they are nowhere near as big as conventional markets. Bitcoin's market capacity of over $9 billion pales by comparison to the New York Stock Exchange's $19 trillion or so. A larger market has more trading, which also helps promote stability.

Still, bitcoin has significant value. Could it offer a significant form of commodity trading much like gold? For now, bitcoin's value simply fluctuates too much. Its volatility may stem from bad press, or exchange problems in the past (see 'The fall of the exchange', Chapter 7), yet even in the most stable periods, cryptocurrencies tend to take sharp dives and jumps in value. As valuable as cryptocurrencies are, they remain more risky than many stocks, and that makes it difficult to convince mainstream investors to ditch conventional markets and put their cash in cryptocurrencies.

Coinlab was another company with a similar business model to BitInstant founded in 2013. The biggest headlines it generated came in 2013 when it formed a partnership with Mt. Gox to process money transfers exclusively in North America, gaining a huge amount of business for Coinlab and potentially opening up the exchange to more customers in the US and Canada. However, only months later Coinlab sued Mt. Gox for breach of contract, claiming the exchange had violated the exclusive right of Coinlab to service Mt. Gox customers in North America when it refused to deliver the customers to Coinlab. It was later revealed that the lawsuit was an attempt to get Mt. Gox to deliver necessary information that Coinlab needed in order to process payments. This issue eventually severed the deal in late 2013, not long before Mt. Gox was forced to shut down permanently.

Bitcoin by post

In an effort to find more customers and create a business model beyond simply buying bitcoins, some companies have begun targeting international remittances as a business model, rather than exchange services – a potentially huge market for cryptocurrencies.

Circle is one company that sees its primary business as money transfers. The company obtained the first **BitLicense** for cryptocurrency-related businesses from New York State, and also an e-money licence from the Financial Conduct Authority in the UK. This allowed Circle to partner with Barclays bank. By utilizing the services of this bank and others in the US, money can be transferred to and from bank accounts in either country via a Circle account. And additionally, one can exchange cryptocurrency into dollars and pounds via a Circle account, which in turn enables direct transfers of the exchange value of cryptocurrency directly into US and UK bank accounts. Circle acts as the intermediary, processing transactions between legitimate bank accounts, as well as the new burgeoning field of cryptocurrency. Circle also recently received a significant amount of funding from Chinese investors, and opened a branch there to potentially allow similar transfers from that country. Abra is a similar app currently only in the Philippines that allows customers to buy and transfer bitcoins to anyone with a phone number.

However, not all bitcoin remittance companies have been successful. For example, a remittance company called Buttercoin had to be shutdown in April 2015 due to lack of investment.

Will signs like this ever be commonplace?

It has also yet to be proved if using bitcoin for remittances is actually any cheaper. In a 2016 report by Citibank reviewed ten common remittance pathways between various countries and found that bitcoin was only cheaper than standard remittance options in one of them – between the US and New Zealand.

Where can you spend cryptocurrency?

The Holy Grail for cryptocurrency enthusiasts has always been the ability to use it in day-to-day transactions as easily as using credit cards or cash. Adoption of cryptocurrency transaction processing by merchants has been slow and sporadic, normally limited to niche industries or online services, or the occasional company owned and run by cryptocurrency enthusiasts. However, this area has perhaps seen the most recent growth, and the companies working on cryptocurrency transaction services are some of the most successful in the cryptocurrency field. They claim that they offer tens of thousands of merchants the ability to accept cryptocurrency for purchases.

BitPay was one of the first companies to offer transaction services for merchants, working with online companies as early as 2011. They helped many of the early adopting companies to accept bitcoin, like Wordpress, Microsoft, and Newegg. After receiving significant investments from Paypal, they expanded their services, working with a company called Gyft to allow users to purchase gift cards with bitcoins that could then be used at retailers. BitPay also began working with Paypal itself, allowing bitcoins to be used to purchase products from Paypal's digital retail platform. In 2016, BitPay launched a VISA debit card that customers could reload using bitcoins, and then use for transactions in normal currency anywhere VISA is accepted.

Coinbase started as an exchange service, but expanded to retail-oriented payment processing. It's also been partnering with Paypal, allowing users to transfer funds exchanged from cryptocurrencies in Coinbase out to a Paypal account.

It's no surprise that Paypal's name keeps coming up. The company handles over $228 billion a year in online transactions, and is considered the primary company for most online money handling in the US. They clearly want to maintain this position, and can afford to take the risks in experimenting with cryptocurrencies, in order to ensure they are not left behind if some method pans out. Although they have primarily invested in other companies and partnered with them for particular service trials, it was recently reported that Paypal itself has applied for patents on integrating cryptocurrency payments into smartphone transactions.

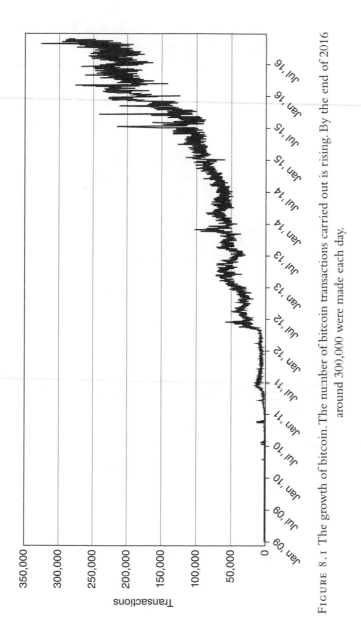

FIGURE 8.1 The growth of bitcoin. The number of bitcoin transactions carried out is rising. By the end of 2016 around 300,000 were made each day.

Although it is now fairly simple for merchants to accept bitcoin, they often don't. There is a chicken-and-egg problem at work – merchants aren't driven to accept cryptocurrencies until their customers demand it, and customers aren't driven to use cryptocurrencies without stores willing to accept it. In the meantime, credit cards and cash continue to be the method of least resistance. And without any particular benefit for choosing to adopt cryptocurrencies over current electronic payments, widespread evolution to a new method seems unlikely.

Free bitcoin for students: How did they spend it?

In October 2014, $100 worth of bitcoins were given to all 4,494 undergraduate students at the Massachusetts Institute of Technology in an experiment to spur acceptance of the cryptocurrency among people who might not otherwise try it. The students were free to do what they wanted with the bitcoins – so long as it was legal. The Boston area boasts a number of shops that accept bitcoin and also had one of the first bitcoin ATMs in the US. In addition, the MIT campus store accepts the currency in exchange for things like textbooks and college sweatshirts. The MIT Bitcoin Project collected data from users to find out how they used their money and whether their attitudes towards the currency had changed.

What was the outcome? Only around 70 per cent of the students signed up for this free cash, and 40 per cent of them traded their bitcoins for money within the first month. After two years, only 14 per cent of the students were still using bitcoin.

Bitcoin accountants

A new domain for cryptocurrency businesses is growing in the field of accounting. Whether one is accepting payments, trading cryptocurrency, or merely buying into bitcoin as an investment, tracking these sorts of transactions is necessary. Because the blockchain and its strings of seemingly random characters and hashes can be confusing, a number of companies are offering to help customers track their cryptocurrency dealings using the blockchain. Libra.tech is one, integrating blockchain analysis into standard accounting procedures. Another company, Contelligence, claims to be working on 'detecting fraudulent transactions' through blockchain analysis, although they give few details as to how.

Whether these services become the answer to a widespread need will be determined by how widespread the use of cryptocurrencies becomes. However, even if there is only a small, core user base for cryptocurrencies, it is likely that these sorts of specialist firms will often provide a much needed niche service. It is ironic that one motivation of virtual currency was to anonymize transactions and prevent authorities from spying on the financial dealings of the currency's users. The reality of the cryptocurrency blockchain is that, as a ledger, it provides highly detailed records of all transactions. And along with this new form of detailed financial record, is a new sort of specialized accountant, trained in the technical details of how to unravel these records and make them legible.

Bitcoin in business

February 2009
Satoshi Nakamoto releases
the bitcoin software for the first time.

April 2010
Laszlo Hanyecz, an early bitcoin enthusiast,
is reportedly the first person to buy anything
with the cryptocurrency when he trades
10,000 bitcoins in exchange for having a
couple of pizzas delivered to his house.

April 2013
Dating website OKCupid
accepts payment in bitcoin.

November 2012
Website database software
provider Wordpress begins
accepting payment in bitcoin.

October 2013
Chinese internet search giant Baidu
accepts bitcoin. Also, Ross Ulbricht
is arrested, and Silk Road shuts down.
It will soon be replaced by a
host of copycat sites.

January 2014
Internet retailers Overstock.com
and TigerDirect accept bitcoin.

November 2015
Coinbase introduces a bitcoin
VISA debit card that can be loaded
with funds using the cryptocurrency
and used anywhere VISA is accepted.

October 2015
BitPay partners with Ingenico to offer
similar point-of-sale bitcoin payments
in the US.

February 2016
Stripe launches a bitcoin payment
integration service for merchants
that connects directly to any
US bank account.

April 2016
BitPay also introduces its own VISA debit
card, allowing over $10,000 of bitcoin
transfers per day with zero fees.

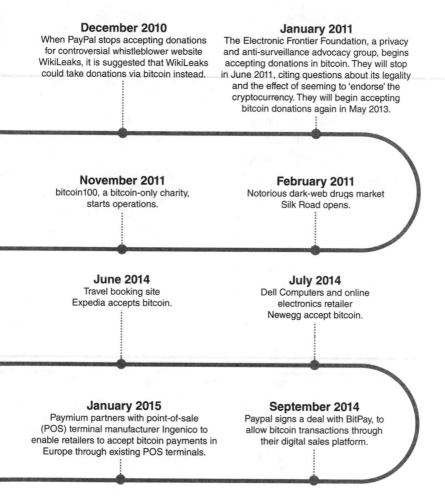

December 2010
When PayPal stops accepting donations for controversial whistleblower website WikiLeaks, it is suggested that WikiLeaks could take donations via bitcoin instead.

January 2011
The Electronic Frontier Foundation, a privacy and anti-surveillance advocacy group, begins accepting donations in bitcoin. They will stop in June 2011, citing questions about its legality and the effect of seeming to 'endorse' the cryptocurrency. They will begin accepting bitcoin donations again in May 2013.

November 2011
bitcoin100, a bitcoin-only charity, starts operations.

February 2011
Notorious dark-web drugs market Silk Road opens.

June 2014
Travel booking site Expedia accepts bitcoin.

July 2014
Dell Computers and online electronics retailer Newegg accept bitcoin.

January 2015
Paymium partners with point-of-sale (POS) terminal manufacturer Ingenico to enable retailers to accept bitcoin payments in Europe through existing POS terminals.

September 2014
Paypal signs a deal with BitPay, to allow bitcoin transactions through their digital sales platform.

Is bitcoin anonymous?

Not really. Getting a bitcoin wallet requires no ID, or even a name. But all transactions can be read in the blockchain. A cryptocurrency changes hands in the open, even if those hands don't have names attached to them.

The blockchain is like the unavoidable 'paper trail' that regular drug dealers try to avoid with money laundering. Drug dealers might earn stacks of cash, but spending it on a house or a car is difficult without it being obvious that money came from illegal sources.

If a particular bitcoin is suspected as having been used to buy drugs on the dark web, one simply has to watch where that bitcoin goes next, tracked through the transaction record of the blockchain. Anyone can follow how it's used. If bitcoin is earned through illegal drug sales, the owner can't be sure that the police are not digitally tracking it. Drug money is no use if it can't ever actually be used.

It is more difficult for law enforcement to discover the identities behind bitcoin transactions than it would be to send a subpoena to a bank as they do for regular currency transactions, but it is certainly not impossible. Those attempting to make use of illicit dark web markets often use 'bitcoin laundering' sites, which mix their bitcoin in with that of a bunch of other users, and then spit it back out on the other side. This complicates matters for authorities, but they are quickly developing tools to track the bitcoin as it passes through any number of exchanges, launderers, and wallets. All the information is in the ledger, it just has to be extracted and traced.

9
Is bitcoin really money?

Bitcoin and other cryptocurrencies certainly have the word 'currency' in their name, but are they really money? Different countries have taken different stances on the question, giving it a variety of legal statuses. But this leads us to a larger question: what exactly is money, anyhow?

A short history of money

If you ask someone about the origin of money, they might tell you a story of how humans once survived by bartering goods – exchanging a chicken for a bushel of wheat, say – until eventually they began to use gold and other precious metals as a common bartering commodity. Gold was universally desirable and non-perishable, which made it ideal as a universal bartering chip. It could be exchanged for anything, or stashed away for a rainy day, therefore fulfilling the first and second defining functions of money – it serves as a medium of exchange and a store of value.

Barter seems like a logical antecedent to money based upon how we currently think money works. However, that story is a myth, promulgated as far back as Ancient Greece. As anthropologists like David Graeber in his book *Debt: The First 5000 Years* (Melville House Publishing, 2011) have shown, there is no evidence that ancient cultures ever used barter exclusively. In fact, the evidence shows that as long as trade has existed, money has been in use. The reason for this is that barter only really works when you are bartering with someone you know and trust. For trading with strangers, an abstract quantity of value is necessary – and that is money.

This was not money in the sense of coins and notes, but an abstract ledger of credit and debt. People kept track of who owed them what and vice versa, in precise, agreed upon units. Money was thus born not as a medium of exchange or a store of value, but as a unit of account – the third function of money, that we often forget in our everyday understandings of it.

Part of the confusion, notes Graeber, is that we have found coins as much as 2,700 years old in archaeological sites, and assume that money only started with this artefact. But in reality, money exists separately from any piece of currency. Money is an abstract idea that existed as far back as the ancient civilizations of Mesopotamia, where writing was also pioneered.

This Roman coin is from around 400 CE, but the first coins
were made 300 years earlier.

As trade networks expand, keeping track of IOUs becomes unwieldy. At that point it makes sense to introduce a physical currency. One of the first organized systems of coinage was created in 8th-century Europe by the emperor Charlemagne, and was based upon silver.

But in fact, there still wasn't much of the actual coinage in existence. What mattered were the units – livres, sous and deniers, the model for many later currencies including pounds, shillings and pence – which were standardized and used to keep track of the exchange of goods, swapped back and forth in ledgers, but rarely changing hands in actual pieces of currency.

The practice of money in ledger form has survived to the current day, sometimes utilizing high technology, and sometimes low technology. The Bank of England still kept track of debits and credits using split sticks of willow wood known as 'tallies' until the mid-19th century. Today, ledgers are sometimes kept in the form of chains of cryptographic hashes.

In medieval Europe, tally sticks like these were used
to record debts and exchanges.

The problem with coins

Emperor Charlemagne's currency was what is called
'commodity money', where the value of the coins was
embodied in the metal they were made from (confusingly,
coins minted from precious metal are called 'specie').

By minting a currency for his realm, Charlemagne was
exercising a right that has been recognized since at least the
3rd century BCE, when the advisors of King Xuan of the
Chinese kingdom of Chu encouraged him to take control
of all currency production for better management. From
that point, it has generally been understood that the sovereign of a region is the primary source of its currency. Even
when minting is outsourced to private interests, they only
mint under the extension of the authority of the sovereign.

This authority could be profitable for the sovereign,
who extracted a 'seigniorage' fee for minting the currency
in the form of a percentage of the precious metal used to
mint the coins. However, it created serious problems for
the wider economy.

Making coinage from precious metals might sound like a simple activity, but in fact it is so complex that it makes blockchain technology sound almost straightforward by comparison.

One well-known problem with coins made from precious metal is that they are 'lossy'. Simply by being handled, coins lose fractions of their weight. Unscrupulous practices can accelerate the losses. Shaving and clipping of coins to steal a fraction of their precious metal, or even shaking the coins in cloth bags to collect the dust that wears off, was a constant problem. Coins lost as much as 10 per cent of their mass, especially if the value of the precious metal was on the increase. These light coins would then have to be reminted at a heavy cost.

Even worse, if the market price for the metal in a coin rose higher than its face value, people had an incentive to melt down the currency and sell it as metal. This also led to a currency shortages and required the mint to make more coins.

A sovereign can always change the value of the coins to be more in line with the price of the metal, called 'crying up' or 'crying down' the currency. But this has the effect of making markets unstable.

These problems are compounded if the currency uses both gold and silver coinage (called a bimetallic standard). Now there are two metal prices that must be considered when trying to stabilize the amount of currency in the system, and users will try to transfer all their money into one metal or the other, depending on the state of each price as compared to the coin value.

The era of gold standards

Because of the intractable problems with specie currency (coins made directly from a precious metal), the next step in the development of money was the bullion standard, more commonly called the gold standard. The contemporary understanding of the gold standard is 'currency backed up by gold', but it was never as simple as that.

Under the bullion standard, the sovereign does not necessarily make coins from a precious metal, but uses a less valuable metal or even paper. These 'token' coins and notes are intrinsically worthless but are backed by a promise to exchange them for bullion 'upon demand'. In other words, somebody in possession of a banknote or coin could in principle turn up at the sovereign's door and demand to exchange it for the equivalent value of gold.

This escaped the clipping and melting issues that dogged specie money. It also meant that the sovereign could issue as many banknotes or coinage as they wanted, as long as they could back them up with their gold reserves.

England officially made the 1819 gold standard functional with the 1821 Coinage Act, which introduced token coins made from less valuable alloys. The US settled on a gold standard in 1879.

Contrary to popular belief, the gold standard did not mean that every unit of currency in circulation was backed by gold in the vaults. Sovereigns could and often did issue more currency than they could back up. However, they couldn't just print and mint as much money as they wanted. The money supply had to be kept in check, otherwise a loss of confidence in the currency could cause a run on the nation's gold reserves as people rushed to convert their worthless tokens into gold. To avert such financial panics, the Bank of England suspended the redemption of currency for gold a number of times in the mid 19th century.

While the gold standard did seem to solve the problem of specie money, creating currency stability, reducing inflation over the long term and creating fixed exchange rates between gold standard countries, it caused dramatic price instability over the short term. The inelastic nature of a currency secured by a nation's gold reserves meant that in times of economic downturn, prices of household goods would sometimes drop by large percentages, and increase by similar amounts during boom times.

Golden age: A gold trader at the Bank of England.

Furthermore, the government's ability to increase its spending was limited by its reserves of bullion. For this reason the US suspended its promise of redemption during the Civil War, minting currency on debt instead.

The same problem eventually drove much of the world off the gold standard for good. The First World War led to the suspension of the gold standard in much of Europe so that governments could produce debt-backed currency to finance their war efforts. The subsequent economic depression of the 1920s caused those nations that attempted to continue or resume the gold standard to back off again. The US ceased redeeming gold for currency to the public in 1933, and in 1971 stopped doing so to the central banks of other countries, formally bringing the gold standard to an end.

Many people still hanker for the supposed certainties of the gold standard, and some have even suggested that cryptocurrencies might be the basis of a new one. Exactly how this would work is not clear, as cryptocurrencies are not backed by precious metal in vaults, which is the defining feature of a gold standard. For now, the age of gold standards is over, and something called 'fiat currency' reigns supreme.

Fiat currencies

Understanding fiat currencies is important because cryptocurrencies have been described as 'post-fiat' currency.

At first glance, fiat currencies defy common sense. Put simply, they are currencies that are valuable simply because the government that issues them says so. The notes and coins in your wallet or pocket are fiat currency, sustained by a collective trust in their value rather than any intrinsic worth. If you took them to the central bank and demanded your gold, you'd be sent packing.

The era of fiat currencies may have been ushered in by war, but they were not invented out of the blue. They evolved along with growing economies and their financial institutions.

A primary challenge for any economy is to have enough money to do business, but not to have too much so that prices undergo inflation, nor too little so that there is deflation. The supply of available money must be in tune with demand for it, or else the value of money itself will fluctuate, not unlike any other product. Regulating the money supply in order to maintain a stable economy has long been recognized as the sovereign's responsibility.

But there are other players in the game. As private banks grew in prominence in 15th- and 16th-century Europe, it was acknowledged that there was a benefit in decentralizing some control of the money supply. By issuing credit to their customers, banks were in effect creating money out of thin air. The money issued through a loan did not come from anywhere. It only existed in the bank's assessment of the customer's ability to repay the loan. By managing this risk in their balance sheet, and doing their business well enough that they could continue to make loans without becoming overwhelmed by bad debt, they were expanding the economy. Often this credit produced by the banks would circulate in readily usable form such as 'promissory notes' – in other words, the banks issued their own currency.

But having freewheeling currencies in circulation was just too difficult for governments to regulate. As good as banks were at managing risk in the good times, panics and economic downturns eventually brought many crashing down. In 1844, England's Bank Charter Act began centralizing the creation of banknotes with the Bank of England. The Free Banking Era in the US, during which any bank could issue their own paper money, was ended in 1864 after one of many economic crashes.

But while sovereigns slowly attained a monopoly on minting, banks continued to magic money out of nothing by making loans. Money creation through credit was too useful for governments to disallow. In fact, they wanted a piece of the action, and so they made their own banks. The Bank of England was created in 1694 to manage the exchange of the nation's currency and to handle the government's debt. After several abortive attempts to create either a national bank or systems of national banks, the US created the Federal Reserve in 1913.

Central banks issue debt to stabilize their fiat currencies. Bonds, the exchangeable notes of this debt, allow the sovereign to expand government spending without increasing the amount of currency in circulation. The bonds bring in currency when they are sold to the customer, which the government can then spend. During an economic downturn, banks can also buy the bonds back from the public, then pushing more currency out into the economy. The central bank's ability to affect the amount of currency in circulation became the most important tool in ensuring that currency's value.

Contrary to popular belief, central banks work today not by printing money, but by what are called 'open market activities'. All other banks in the country are required to keep an account with a certain percentage of their holdings at the central bank, in order to guarantee that they are solvent. By changing the interest rate on those accounts, or by making short-term trades of bonds for cash to those accounts, the central bank is able to control the amount of currency the banks have at their disposal – which is the amount of money they can loan to customers – and which, in effect, is the amount of money in general circulation. In the contemporary age of money, it is not the number of physical banknotes in existence that defines the money supply, but the amount available on banks' ledgers with the central bank. The total amount of money, including these central bank balances, is many times greater than the amount of currency (3.35 times greater in the US, as of June 2016).

The days of old-fashioned banks could be numbered.

Private currencies

Today we live in an era of fiat money where the sovereign has exclusive power to make currency within a nation state. However, that has not stopped people – including cryptocurrency designers – from attempting to flout that authority.

Such attempts usually end up being stamped out under counterfeiting laws. US federal law on forgery and counterfeiting makes it illegal for anyone to make their own currency. The maximum penalty is five years in prison. But the law hasn't stopped people from trying.

In 2007 a man named Angel Cruz attempted to launch 'The US Private Dollar', and began paying employees with checks that drew on this currency. Banks promptly rejected them for not having correct bank codes printed on them. He claimed that the currency was backed by over $300 billion of its 'members" assets but did not elaborate on who or what these were. After a bizarre episode in which Cruz and his supporters attempted to 'evict' the staff of a Bank of America branch in Florida, claiming the fictitious 'The United Cities Private Court' had authorized him to do so, he was indicted by the federal government with conspiracy to defraud the US, as well as bank fraud. However, he was not charged with any crime of forgery, or relating to the currency itself. Cruz fled before trial, and is still on the run.

Another notorious case was perhaps closer to actually making a currency. In 2006, a group calling itself National Organization for the Repeal of the Federal Reserve Act and the Internal Revenue Code (NORFED) began issuing 'Liberty Dollars' minted out of silver and gold, along with paper notes. This currency looked not unlike US currency, which quickly drew the ire of federal officials. The US Mint issued a press release warning against the currency because of what they described as 'confusing' and 'misleading' similarities to genuine US currency.

While selling a medallion of precious metal is not a crime, the goal of NORFED was to have its coins widely accepted by merchants as de facto legal tender. The physical similarities between US currency and the Liberty Dollars, with the design's intention to mislead, were the undoing of the scheme. The Secret Service and FBI seized the stock of Liberty Dollars, and Bernard von NotHaus, the creator of NORFED, was convicted of violating the law against minting currency, and other anti-counterfeiting statutes.

This court case played out from 2009 to 2011, and early bitcoin enthusiasts kept abreast of developments. Bitcoin, while having its own libertarian proponents that sympathized with the political goals of NORFED, had a few things going for it that Liberty Dollars did not.

Virtual currencies

Another type of private currency is virtual currency, which consists solely of data on computer systems. For that reason virtual currencies are quite similar to cryptocurrencies, and worth exploring – though there are important differences.

One example of a virtual currency is Linden Dollars, the unit of exchange in the online virtual game Second Life. Linden Labs, the creator of Second Life, is the sole creator of that currency and is directly responsible for its use. The terms of service for Second Life state that Linden Dollars have no value outside of the game. The currency always remains the property of the company, and there are no guarantees to it or its value. In this way Linden Labs maintains control and responsibility, including preventing the use of Linden Dollars for anything illegal.

The 'gold' used in the massive multiplayer online game World of Warcraft is similar. Blizzard, the company running the game, insist that the currency has no real value, and players caught trading any in-game items for real-world money are permanently banned. Another online multiplayer game, EVE Online, allows players to buy

---

in-game currency with real money, but bars it from being converted in the other direction.

Some virtual currency systems have been set up outside of video game environments, but have invariably ended up falling afoul of the law. E-gold was a website launched in 1996 that allowed users to transfer a digital currency (called E-gold) between themselves, denominated in grams of gold or other precious metals. While the US Internal Revenue Service (IRS) determined that E-gold did not fall under the definition of currency, the service was characterized as being tailor-made for criminals, and was shut down by the US government in 2008. Liberty Reserve (not to be confused with Liberty Dollars) operated a similar service; it was shut down in 2013.

Despite both existing only inside computer systems and using cryptography to secure their transactions, there are some crucial differences between virtual currencies and cryptocurrencies.

The main one is that virtual currencies do not use a blockchain ledger or any form of proof-of-work. Without a blockchain, virtual currencies must be produced and managed by a single business or institution. There is no authority responsible for cryptocurrencies' use, and no one to enforce rules other than those provided for in the cryptocurrency programming. There are no Terms of Service other than the open-source licence of the software. They are also much more difficult to ban: thanks largely to activists such as the Electronic Frontier Foundation, software publishing is protected as free speech by the First Amendment. The only way to 'ban' a cryptocurrency would be to remove every instance of the software from the network.

So what is cryptocurrency, legally?

From our exploration of the nature and history of money, it seems clear that cryptocurrency does not conform exactly to any past or current definition of money. Exactly what it is, though, still remains up in the air, as judgments by government authorities have shown.

Various regulatory agencies of governments around the world have been evolving in their treatment of cryptocurrency, and are continuing to do so. This evolution shows a slowly growing acceptance; however, there is nervousness about making sure that cryptocurrency has the appropriate status – either as currency, commodity, or property.

In the US, the evolution began in the courts. In August 2013, a US federal judge wrote: 'Bitcoin can be used as money,' in deciding that a Securities and Exchange Commission (SEC) suit against Bitcoin Savings & Trust, a Bitcoin-based Ponzi scheme, could proceed. The SEC did not claim that bitcoin was money but it charged that, regardless of what bitcoin was, Bitcoin Savings & Trust had been selling fraudulent securities and was therefore breaking the law.

Not a week later, the New York State Department of Financial Services issued subpoenas to 22 companies working with bitcoin in an effort to learn exactly how these companies ran their businesses. The primary concern of the authorities was how to prevent the use of cryptocurrencies in money laundering, either for illicit purchases such as those on the dark web marketplace Silk Road, or for money transfers related to terrorism. Some of these investigations led to fines, or changes in the way that these companies managed their customers.

But despite the unsavoury reputation that cryptocurrencies earned in 2013 and 2014 due to the court cases against Silk Road, BitInstant, and Mt. Gox, it appears that US government officials were not opposed to cryptocurrencies as an idea. Although the FBI had produced an intelligence assessment in 2012 entitled, 'Bitcoin Virtual Currency: Unique Features Present Distinct Challenges for Deterring Illicit Activity', when the FBI arrested Silk Road's founder Ross Ulbricht in October 2013, the criminal complaint explicitly set the nature of cryptocurrencies aside from the crime itself, noting that they had legitimate uses. A month later, the Senate held hearings on cryptocurrencies. The findings were positive, stating that cryptocurrencies may have 'profound and exciting implications' for the future of finance.

In 2014, the IRS added some clarity by issuing an official notice on the legal status of cryptocurrencies. The tax agency came to the conclusion that cryptocurrencies were not, in fact, currencies, but 'property'. The selling of cryptocurrencies would be taxed like the sale of any other property – like company stock, for example. This neatly sidestepped the awkward issue of deciding how a decentralized cryptocurrency might fit into the government's monetary policy, and instead classified it as a strange, digital financial instrument.

For the time being, that settled the issue in the US. Cryptocurrencies are legal; not only that, they can be taxed. They are not legal tender, but can be 'used as money'.

However, other countries came to different conclusions. In September 2014, the UK's HM Revenue and Customs (HMRC) specified that for corporate tax, bitcoin is to be considered a currency. Therefore, they argued, no special rules are necessary, and any profits or losses based on currency exchange are taxed as normal. This applies for standard income tax, as well as capital gains tax. HMRC put off the question of collecting VAT (sales tax) for purchases of bitcoin, deferring to the decisions of the EU, but did note that for purchases of goods made with bitcoin, VAT should be collected in the equivalent value of Pounds Sterling, as normal.

In October 2015, the European Court of Justice upheld this reasoning, and declared that purchases of bitcoin on exchanges are tax-free, because it is similar in nature to 'currency, banknotes and coins used as legal tender'. This philosophy is wholly different from the perspective of authorities in the US.

In other countries things are different yet again. Argentina, Bangladesh, Bolivia, Ecuador, Indonesia, Thailand and Vietnam have all made some aspect of cryptocurrencies illegal. In China, bitcoin is hugely popular, but authorities banned financial institutions from transmitting funds to business involving bitcoin. This doesn't ban cryptocurrencies, themselves, but does make their use more difficult.

It is only to be expected that laws and official guidance on cryptocurrencies will continue to evolve as the technology does. There are no laws yet about the legality of 'smart contracts' or other novel blockchain technologies that have been proposed and developed by companies such as Ethereum (see 'Smart contracts' and 'The age of Ethereum', Chapter 12). What new, future offspring will branch off from the blockchain, no one – least of all the lawmakers – can predict.

Okay, so are cryptocurrencies money or not?

In the sense that cryptocurrencies are an abstract unit that can be used as a token of exchange by anyone with a computer, they are, by most definitions, money.

However, they do not cohere to the modern, global economic definition of the function of currency. They are not under the mandate of any sovereign government. There is no way for any entity to control them using monetary policy. With a hard limit on most cryptocurrencies' total supply, they are deflationary by design. While that is good if one holds a large amount of deflationary currency as an investment, from an economic perspective it is less than ideal because it tends to discourage spending and investment in new business ventures. One of a currency's main functions is as a medium of exchange, not just to sit in a bank vault.

As a throwback to an archaic system of bullion (or gold) standards, cryptocurrencies still fail as money. They are not backed by precious metal holdings, and they are not a precious commodity against which a currency can be issued. Nor are they specie, as they are not minted by a sovereign authority withdrawing a fee in order to manage the production of a money supply.

Even in the most basic banking functionalities, they fail to be money. There is no way to issue a loan in cryptocurrency kept on a bank's books, without actually transferring cryptocurrency. The creation of money through credit, the lynchpin of financial technology since the Renaissance period, is impossible.

On the plus side, cryptocurrencies take one aspect of money's existence – the idea of an abstract unit tallied in a ledger – and make it a concrete reality. However, the blockchain is, in a sense, too exacting a ledger. The exact number of cryptocurrency units in existence is the only cryptocurrency that can be used. Money has never worked like that. Between abstract money and concrete currency is the slippery area where credit can be created, markets expanded, and the elasticity of monetary policy can back up the global economy.

It is far better to think of cryptocurrency as a new sort of financial instrument. Exacting in its accounting, digitally concrete via cryptography, it can be moved and traded as a digital store of value, used in lieu of money in certain circumstances, but never likely to displace money as the foundational measure of a wide, diverse economy.

A brief history of money

4000 BCE
Correspondence counters are used in
Mesopotamia to tally equivalent quantities
and values of particular commodities.

6th century BCE
Awards in Ancient Greek athletic
competitions were measured in
units of currency.

16th century CE
Private debit and credit markets
become standard throughout
European marketplaces.

14th century CE
Cheques are commonly used
in southern Europe.

1694
The Bank of England is chartered, to
manage the debt of the government.

1717
Isaac Newton creates
UK's de facto gold standard
by forcing all silver currency
out of existence.

1921
Fox, Fowler, and Co, the last
private bank in England still
permitted to issue its own
banknotes, ceases to mint currency.

1914
The outbreak of the First World War
causes UK and many other European
countries to vacate the gold standard.

1925–31
UK briefly adopts a gold
exchange standard, only to cease
as massive amounts of gold
depart the country.

1933
President Franklin Roosevelt
nationalizes gold within the US,
and ceases making payments in gold,
effectively departing the gold standard.

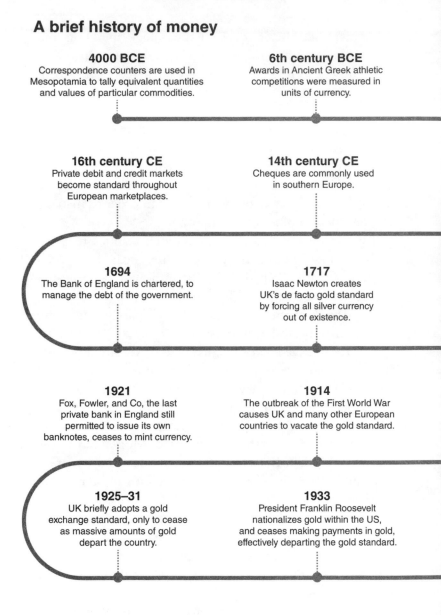

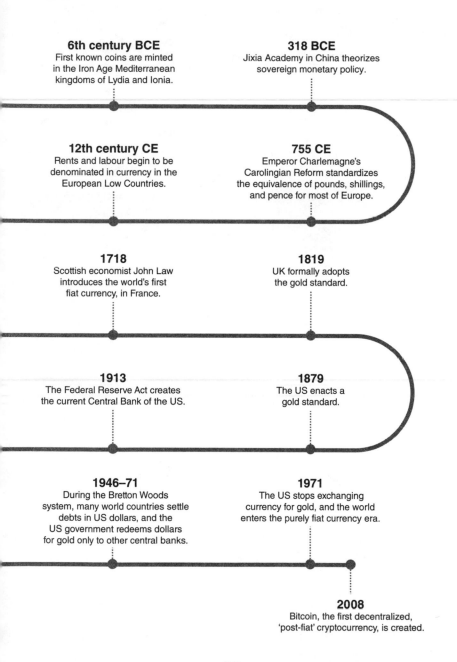

6th century BCE
First known coins are minted in the Iron Age Mediterranean kingdoms of Lydia and Ionia.

318 BCE
Jixia Academy in China theorizes sovereign monetary policy.

12th century CE
Rents and labour begin to be denominated in currency in the European Low Countries.

755 CE
Emperor Charlemagne's Carolingian Reform standardizes the equivalence of pounds, shillings, and pence for most of Europe.

1718
Scottish economist John Law introduces the world's first fiat currency, in France.

1819
UK formally adopts the gold standard.

1913
The Federal Reserve Act creates the current Central Bank of the US.

1879
The US enacts a gold standard.

1946–71
During the Bretton Woods system, many world countries settle debts in US dollars, and the US government redeems dollars for gold only to other central banks.

1971
The US stops exchanging currency for gold, and the world enters the purely fiat currency era.

2008
Bitcoin, the first decentralized, 'post-fiat' cryptocurrency, is created.

10
The returns and departures of Satoshi Nakamoto

Bitcoin's creator has long been a mystery. Recently there have been some prime suspects... An unlikely suspect made headlines as he attempted to claim the title. But the mystery only deepened.

The man who would not be Nakamoto

The 6 March 2014 edition of *Newsweek* contained what seemed like a major scoop. Journalist Leah McGrath Goodman had done the impossible: she had discovered the true identity of Satoshi Nakamoto. And not only that, there was an incredible twist: the man's name was *actually* Satoshi Nakamoto!

At least officially, his name was Satoshi Nakamoto. The 64-year old physicist went by Dorian Nakamoto. He had a career perhaps not untypical for someone living in the Inland Empire metropolis of Southern California – working for a number of aerospace and other high tech firms, including a brief stint working on classified electronics systems for a government contractor, and for the US Federal Aviation Administration.

Perhaps it was this technical background that inspired Goodman to trek to California to meet this particular Nakamoto. And there, in the presence of two police officers that Nakamoto had called when she knocked on his door, he uttered the sentences that caused a media circus to spring up around him:

> 'I am no longer involved in that and I cannot discuss it,' he says, dismissing all further queries with a swat of his left hand. 'It's been turned over to other people. They are in charge of it now. I no longer have any connection.'

Taking this quote, Goodman went to interview a number of Nakamoto's relatives, who did not confirm or deny the claim, but provided additional quotes to the support the theory that he was smart, secretive, and leaned towards the libertarian side of politics.

The next day, swarms of reporters arrived at Nakamoto's house. After telling them that he would speak with the first reporter that bought him lunch, he hopped into the car of an Associated Press reporter. Several other reporters gave chase, tailing them to a nearby restaurant. Meanwhile, the local sheriff attempted to maintain order outside the Nakamoto home, as the horde of the press maintained vigil.

But it was all for nothing. Dorian Nakamoto denied that he was that Satoshi. He claimed that his statement, the best proof that he had something to do with bitcoin, was a misunderstanding. He had thought Goodman was talking about his classified work for the government. This was also the reason for his unease when she showed up at his door – he knew he was unable to talk about that work, and did not want to be harassed by journalists. A week later, Nakamoto began taking donations for a threatened lawsuit against *Newsweek*. The magazine published a statement written by him at the end of their original article, in which he denied that he had anything to do with bitcoin. And perhaps the most substantial stroke came the day after the article was released – the P2P Foundation user account used by the real Satoshi Nakamoto, one of the sources of the original bitcoin whitepaper, came back to life after years of silence. 'I am not Dorian Nakamoto', the account posted simply.

Dorian Nakamoto vehemently denied having anything to do with bitcoin.

Eventually, the circus died down, until the next candidate for the real identity of Satoshi Nakamoto would be proposed. It was an honest mistake, perhaps. Given the curiosity over the mysterious pseudonym, it was maybe only a matter of time until a completely uninvolved individual ended up mistakenly in the media's crossfire. And so, the mystery only deepens.

The real Satoshi Nakamoto?

In December 2015, the publications *Wired* and *Gizmodo* announced a major story – they had received a tip about the real identity of Satoshi Nakamoto. Those who kept up with the never ending saga mostly shrugged. After the controversies surrounding many of the other supposed unmaskings of the creator of bitcoin, including the infamous car chase of reporters tailing an unrelated man named Dorian Nakamoto around Los Angeles suburbs, the public was perhaps a bit jaded.

While previous 'unmaskings' of Nakamoto's identity have mostly been educated guesses with no real evidence, *Wired* and *Gizmodo* had some evidence – of a kind. A tipster had delivered pages of emails allegedly written by an Australian named Craig Wright. The emails discussed creating the cryptocurrency in some detail with a colleague named David Kleiman, who had died two years previously. Wright was relatively unknown within the cryptocurrency community, though he had recently been in trouble with the Australian Tax Office. Wright did not publicly respond to the suggestion that he was Nakamoto, other than with a brief denial.

Six months later in May 2016, the trail grew hot again. Wright now publicly claimed to be Satoshi Nakamoto and said he could prove it. Never before had someone both been accused of being Nakamoto, and *also* claimed it was true. The next month, journalist Andrew O'Hagan wrote a long article in the *London Review of Books* giving the inside story and clearing up some of the hazy details. Though certainly not all.

According to O'Hagan, in late 2015 he had received a call from an entertainment lawyer asking him if he wanted to write the life story of the creator of bitcoin. It seemed that Wright was planning on coming forward in parallel with applying for a host of blockchain-related patents under a company called nTrust. Wright would be revealed as the creator of cryptocurrency, the patents would be approved, nTrust would license the patents, and Wright and nTrust would be rich – helping Wright out of his financial and business difficulties. O'Hagan agreed to document the events, but only as a journalist, not as a hired writer.

Over the next six months O'Hagan had many conversations with Wright. Through his *London Review of Books* piece, O'Hagan paints a portrait of a man whose life is certainly entwined with bitcoin. Wright is proficient on the details of the cryptocurrency. He described a collaboration with his friend David Kleiman that mirrored the history of bitcoin exactly. And his somewhat paranoid personality and description of potentially shady business dealings with the world of offshore finance lent credence to his drastic attempts to maintain his anonymity.

But there were pieces missing. Wright's stories often seemed circular, fraught with passion and uncertainty. Emails important to his rendition of the story that he claimed to have were never shown.

O'Hagan was left confused. Was Wright confused himself after spending so many years clinging to anonymity? Or was perhaps the whole thing was some sort of incredibly elaborate ruse?

The story climaxed in May, 2016, when Wright gathered journalists and experts to inspect a blog post he had written, which claimed to present proof that he was Nakamoto. For years, it was known exactly what this proof should look like. Only the true creator of bitcoin would have the secret key that signed the so-called 'genesis block' – the very first block in the chain.

But again, there were pieces missing. In the blog post, Wright used what he claimed was Nakamoto's secret key to sign a message. Upon further inspection, it was clear that Wright had actually just used a public hash of Nakamoto's, which anyone might have found on the internet. Although he claimed it was a mistake, Wright never fixed it.

Many cryptographic experts and bitcoin aficionados began to doubt Wright's claims. In response, Wright offered to do something equally impressive – he would move some of the bitcoins mined during the very early days of the cryptocurrency. It has never been transferred, and it is widely believed to belong to whomever is Satoshi Nakamoto. These bitcoins are held in a trust until 2020, according to Wright, but he would get special permission to move them for the purposes of the demonstration. He never did this, either.

The media circus departed, again finding nothing but disappointment where they expected Nakamoto. But O'Hagan was left wondering, why? Why would Wright set up such an elaborate scam – faking emails, creating stories of relationships and work that never happened – only to trap himself against something he knew he could not deliver? Wright claimed to O'Hagan that he had lost his nerve. He said he was afraid that if he proved he was Nakamoto, he would be arrested for drug trafficking or terrorism charges due to something someone had done with the cryptocurrency after he invented it. O'Hagan described this fear as certainly a real risk, but still, it is just one more riddle in a maze of riddles.

According to most cryptocurrency followers, the mystery of Satoshi Nakamoto is still unsolved.

II

Revamping bitcoin – and the rise of altcoins

Bitcoin could be in trouble. It can't keep up with the number of transactions. Will any of the proposed solutions be successful, or will one of the growing number of alternative cryptocurrencies take over?

Bitcoin's growing problems

Bitcoin has a problem. It cannot get big enough. The crypto-currency is facing problems of scale that Nakamoto didn't envision, as the number of users increase and the blockchain grows longer.

As new transactions are reported to the blockchain, they are compiled to form a new block and written to the blockchain every ten minutes or so. However, the block size is limited. Only 1 MB of transactions can be written every ten minutes. This limits bitcoin to an average of seven transactions per second. That sounds like a lot, but VISA's payment network can process 24,000 transactions per second. Baked into the code of bitcoin is a limitation that means it could never rival a major credit card system, no matter how popular it gets.

Many bitcoin developers, such as Gavin Andresen, the ring-leader of the Bitcoin Core development group, want to fix this problem by making the block size larger. Andresen created an update called bitcoin XT, which would increase the block size to 8 MB, and double the size again on a revolving basis.

But bitcoin has a second problem. It is decentralized, and so even the core developers have no control over what software is being used. If a computer on the network is using bitcoin XT, it will create blocks that are 8 MB. But a computer running the previous version of the software won't be able to understand a block that big. It will only understand blocks created by the older version, and it will continue to create 1 MB blocks itself. This will lead to a situation called a **'fork'**.

A fork, typically a term used to describe when the develop-ment of programming code splits into two separate versions that are no longer identical or compatible, in this case refers to the blockchain itself. There would be two versions of the blockchain – one made and recognized as valid by the bitcoin XT computers, the other used by the original software version. These blockchains would no longer cohere. Such a state would be chaos, of course. The bitcoin network, kept together only by its single, canonical blockchain, would cease to exist. Bitcoin would be split into two different cryptocurrencies, effectively.

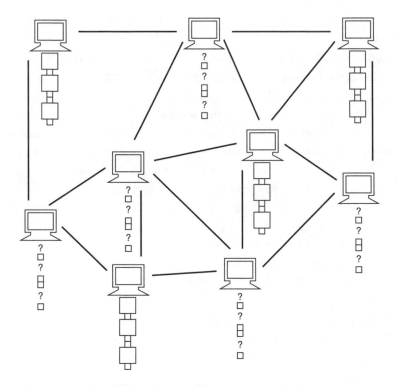

FIGURE II.I Two different halves of the same network. One produces a blockchain that includes both small blocks and big blocks. The other side sees the same blockchain, except that it cannot see the big blocks, only the small blocks. Therefore, it creates a second blockchain, without any big blocks at all.

To prevent a disastrous fork, the software update is designed to wait until a certain date, and then poll the network. If at that time, 75 per cent of the network or more is using bitcoin XT, then it will consider it 'accepted' and switch to the larger blocks. 75 per cent is considered large enough of a majority, that it would force the laggards to update as well, in order to continue to use bitcoin services provided by exchanges and other services. The network votes.

When the software 'voted' in January 2016, only 10 per cent of the network was using the update. The reasons were varied. Some bitcoin users didn't like the update from a technical basis, arguing that there were better ways of fixing the block size problem. Others didn't like the way that the update was 'forced' onto bitcoin, and argued against it as a matter of principle. This debate drew in a number of powerful figures and companies into both sides of the debate. And then, it seems a hacker-for-hire began attacking computers running bitcoin XT, taking them offline. Many companies and individuals rolled back to the previous version just to avoid being attacked.

A possible fix: Segregated witness

The block size is still a problem, but there is a novel solution in the works to help fix it. And the fundamental cleverness of this fix is that there is no possibility of a fork, and therefore a vote like bitcoin XT's is not necessary.

The disjunction between bitcoin XT and bitcoin is known as a 'hard fork', but a 'soft fork' is possible as well. Whereas a hard fork introduces incompatible differences between the new version and the old version, essentially splitting the crypto-currency in two, a soft fork changes the cryptocurrency but still allows communication between older versions and newer versions of the software. The software update is backwards compatible – computers that do not upgrade do not get shut out of the network, they merely do not benefit from the upgrade.

Is there a fork in the road ahead for bitcoin?

It was originally thought that to increase the block size, a hard fork would be necessary. But this new update strategy, known as '**Segregated Witness**', gets around the problem. Rather than increasing the size of the block to accommodate more transactions, it decreases the size of the transaction by reducing the amount of information reported to the blockchain. All the cryptographic information that signs the transactions – ensuring that the cryptocurrency can only be moved by the person holding the secret key to a particular wallet – is kept in a separate tree of information. Once their credentials are approved, a very short message is sent to the blockchain, along with the transaction. This is where the name 'Segregated Witness' or 'SegWit' comes from: the cryptography that witnesses that the signatures are legitimate is kept separate from the blockchain. The Witness merely gives the blockchain a cryptographic 'thumbs up', and then the transaction proceeds. By drastically shortening the amount of information reported to the blockchain, it is estimated that SegWit could enable nearly four times as many transactions per block as are currently possible.

The real benefit, is that computers running an older version of the bitcoin software won't see the 'thumbs up' from SegWit, but they will continue to see the transactions in the blockchain. They will appear strange — bitcoins that apparently appear out of thin air, without any signature. But because these strange, magical bitcoins can only be added if the SegWit part of the network allows them, they will continue to be just as secure. So, even if only a portion of the network runs SegWit, the overall network will still benefit from the improved efficiency. A larger block size might still be necessary, but this improved efficiency will give bitcoin some much needed breathing room. In late 2016, the rate of bitcoin transactions was edging up to around 2,000 per block, and an average of about 3.3 per second — or in other words, running at about half capacity. Those who see a bright future for bitcoin would like this capacity to be expanded as soon as possible.

But the developers working on the SegWit updates think that other improvements in the software will make it attractive for computers in the network to update. Transactions will be faster overall. And most importantly, SegWit has the benefit of solving the 'transaction malleability' problem, that was blamed for the collapse of Mt. Gox in 2014 (see 'The transaction malleability problem', Chapter 7). That error occurred when a slight alteration in signatures caused a transaction on the blockchain to have a different ID than expected. Because signatures are moved into the SegWit, transaction IDs are now completely different, and this malleability is no longer possible. Proponents argue that being free from this well-known vulnerability alone will be motivation to users to update their software.

But that remains to be seen. In July 2016, the SegWit code was going through its review period. After that, it will be made available to the network. Only then will the network decide which course it wants to take.

The Lightning Network

Not everyone is convinced that the block size problem is really a problem. A new idea, called the **Lightning Network**, may make the entire issue moot.

Lightning could save bitcoin.

Rather than try and cram thousands of transactions per second into the blockchain, the Lightning Network takes a contrary approach – keeping many transactions *off* the blockchain.

The idea is best described in terms of small, repeated payments. One user authorizes a certain amount of cryptocurrency for transactions with another particular user — like opening a subscription account with a down payment. That transaction remains open, only shared between those two users. Over time, many incremental transactions are recorded, sending bitcoins one way or the other, until finally the authorized down payment amount is used up. Then, the transaction closes, and is sent to the blockchain. It is only recorded in the blockchain once, as a single transaction, even though there were any number of smaller transactions that were summed up into that single transaction.

As an example, imagine buying a coffee every day for a month. Instead of notifying the blockchain after every transaction, the Lightning Network allows the buyer and the coffee shop to just report the total transaction at the end of the month, whilst still maintaining security.

The way it remains secure is that each incremental transaction must be approved by each user. If at any time they fail to agree, the process is stopped, the totals from before the disagreement are returned to each user, and the information is logged to the blockchain. Because the transaction is only occurring between these two users, their simultaneous agreement or disagreement can be logged immediately. The level of risk is low, because only a small amount of cryptocurrency can be put into this open transaction at a time, and each step along the way must have both parties' agreement.

The Lightning Network is only an experiment as of mid-2016, and a lot of the details have yet to be worked out. As well, it would require SegWit or some update like it to fix the transaction malleability issue. It would also require some additional technological tricks that are only theoretical at the moment.

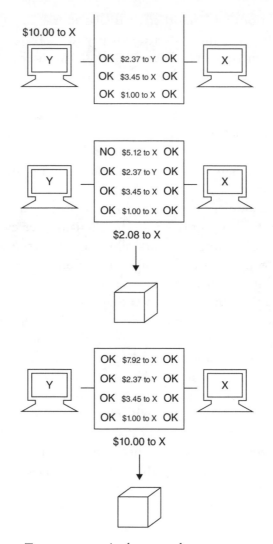

FIGURE 11.2 Two computers in the network open up a transaction, like a small box. Little by little, transactions add up within it until it uses up the entire value of the transaction, and then it is closed, and sent to the network. Each mini transaction appears as a small agreement, requiring both computers' consent.

The Lightning Network and other innovative ideas show that, although bitcoin is several years old, its evolution is continuing. The cryptocurrency may change beyond recognition, depending on what sort of alternations the distributed network decides to accept.

The world's biggest crypto-economy

In mid-2013, while US companies were struggling to ease the process of transferring money into Mt. Gox so that customers could buy bitcoins, a Chinese exchange named BTC China set up a deal with mobile services provider Tencent. For the first time, Chinese citizens could transfer money directly into a bitcoin exchange. Within a few months, in November 2013, bitcoin hit its highest price ever, trading for as much as $1,242. Chinese interest in bitcoin exploded.

The Chinese bitcoin bubble would eventually burst when the government issued a warning that it was illegal for banks to transfer Chinese yuan directly to a cryptocurrency business. This meant that after only a few months Tencent had to cease its service with BTC China, cooling the public's interest. But the Chinese appetite for cryptocurrencies had been whetted, and eventually China would grow to represent the vast majority of exchange trading volume and mining, and likely a large percentage of bitcoin ownership as well.

In 2016, two Chinese exchanges, Huobi and OKCoin, were responsible for 92 percent of bitcoin trading. The top four mining pools, with 76 per cent of the global hashrate, are based and owned in China. Some have attempted to explain the Chinese passion for bitcoin as a way around Chinese currency controls. Chinese law states that individuals cannot send more than $50,000 worth of yuan out of the country per year. But Chinese bitcoin investors deny this – they say that the currency controls already have plenty of loopholes, and they believe that the Chinese are into bitcoin purely from an investment standpoint. China has a strong culture of gambling, and the large boom and bust cycles of bitcoin are attractive to people looking for a big payoff.

Additionally, it must be noted that China has more experience with unconventional payment methods. While Europeans and Americans might have balked at the apparent insecurity of using a phone as a method of payment, in China ad hoc payment arrangements were already commonplace. By as early as 2012, online payments in China represented over $660 billion, and grew to $1.3 trillion in 2015. Today, Alipay claims 400 million active users, and Tencent's WeChat Pay smartphone based payment system has over 300 million users. While in other parts of the world the unfamiliar aspects of cryptocurrencies might make users take pause, in China things are different.

As bitcoin looks to be in China to stay, the Chinese government is considering revisions that would enable wider use of cryptocurrencies. Like the US government, they seem primed to acknowledge bitcoin as a commodity, rather than a currency.

Outside of China, cryptocurrency proponents are worried about what Chinese interest will do to the cryptocurrency itself. Control of mining is a de facto control of the network, in terms of 'voting' for new software updates. With 76 per cent of the processing power of the network, these mining pools control 76 per cent of the vote. But while the effective 'decentralized' control of bitcoin is quite lopsided, it seems that for now, it is unified around the idea of ensuring the cryptocurrency stays valuable and relevant.

The altcoin explosion

As soon as bitcoin began taking off in 2011, there were people who were discontented at the cryptocurrency's newfound popularity. Mining became more difficult, prices started to increase, and weaknesses started to emerge. But if one cryptocurrency worked, why not two? Or ten? Soon there were hundreds of 'altcoins' that formed a complex cryptocurrency market system.

The joke cryptocurrency

When a cryptocurrency emerged based upon the popular meme called 'doge' certainly no one could say they expected it. The meme is a cute Shiba Inu dog with a peculiar expression on its face surrounded by colourful captions, not immediately anything to do with cryptocurrency.

Around the end of 2013, Adobe Systems employee Jackson Palmer was watching the excitement around altcoins unfold. He decided to make a 'Dogecoin' website as a joke. Billy Markus, a software developer, found the site, liked the idea and got in touch with Palmer. They altered the source code of litecoin a little, mostly changing the look of the software to mimic the doge meme. They also made the block award random — anywhere from zero to one million dogecoins were awarded every time a block was solved, though this would be changed in time — and made the total amount of coins limitless. After all, it was a joke. Why not make it fun?

But dogecoins actually took off. Maybe it was the oddity of the random block awards, or maybe it was the

---

novelty of a coin with such high quantities that one could actually own whole numbers, rather than the small fractions of bitcoin most people could afford. Or perhaps it was simply that cute animals are always a strong currency on the internet.

Dogecoin might not be the most powerful alterna tive cryptocurrency. There are so many, that one dogecoin traded for the equivalent of two hundredths of one US cent in July 2016. But overall, the cryptocurrency is worth a total of about $24.8 million today. Users have continued mining them, and they are often used online as tokens of minuscule recognition, such as being given as a 'tip' for good posts on a website. Dogecoin are lighthearted and fun as opposed to the seriousness and dark web–intrigue of bitcoin.

The first altcoin to succeed was litecoin. It was not the first modification of bitcoin to be tried, but for some reason, it is the one that was most successful. Its mechanism is almost identical to bitcoin's except that it had a block time of just 2½ minutes, instead of bitcoin's ten-minute block, to speed up transactions.

In October 2011 when litecoin was launched, graphics processing units (**GPU**) were taking over bitcoin mining, making it difficult for users running bitcoin software on their own computers' central processing unit (**CPU**) to mine any bitcoins. Litecoin's hashing algorithm, called scrypt, could not initially be hashed using GPUs, which slowed down the mining arms race. Since that time, scrypt-based GPU software and ASICs have been developed, but this factor initially boosted the popularity of litecoin by making it seem more democratic, unlike the high-stakes mining of bitcoins. Once litecoin gained popularity, it served as a good alternative to bitcoin, allowing investors to hedge their cryptocurrency investments against the wild price fluctuations driven by bitcoin's ongoing legal dramas.

After the success of litecoin, many new coins were launched with the hope of becoming the next second-place-to-bitcoin. If investors and miners got in early on an altcoin that made it big, it would be like getting in on bitcoin back in the early days. Creators would often launch new coins with very subtle variations, in the hope that their version would become just valuable enough that their early mining would allow them to cash in once the altcoin had a wider user base. By taking the source code from any previously released cryptocurrency and making a few changes, a whole new altcoin could be created in minutes.

With this explosion of possibilities for getting rich quick in cryptocurrency, the altcoin market was soon transformed into a penny stock marketplace. In 2013, as the number of exchanges trading cryptocurrency increased rapidly, many exchanges would attempt to draw customers by introducing new and untested cryptocurrencies. As newly introduced alt-coins hit the exchanges, they quickly exploded into bubbles that often deflated rapidly. In these quick price increases, one could rapidly make 100 per cent on an investment or more. And, one could just as easily lose that investment. Like 'penny stocks', risky investments worth just a few cents that allow an investor to easily double or triple their money, the altcoin mar-kets became a fast paced world of rumour, hype, and strike-it-rich schemes.

A common scheme was for altcoin creators to secretly mine their coin for weeks before announcing it to the general public. By the time others started mining and the hype took off, the creators had already sacked away a cache of the currency, which they could then dump on the market when they wanted to cash out. This scheme was named 'pre-mining'. Another strategy was for an investor, called a 'whale', to buy a huge amount of a newly listed altcoin in order to drive up the price. Then, as the price rose and others began buying in to try and take advantage of the increasing price, the whale would liquidate their holdings, earning as much profit as they could while simultaneously driving down the price. Just like in the stock market, this was called a 'pump-and-dump'.

Bitcoin was hitting its all-time high prices in late 2013 as Silk Road was shut down and the popular consensus was beginning to believe that cryptocurrencies could be used for legitimate means. Meanwhile, investors were also taking bigger risks with altcoins that would rocket to popularity only to fall immediately. Mining fluctuated rapidly as new exchanges listed or delisted the altcoins, or as interest simply waned. Some altcoins were around for only a period of months, others merely for weeks.

However, the altcoin markets as a whole had the effect of propping up bitcoin. When an altcoin is added to an exchange, the very first thing it can be traded for is bitcoin – not dollars, yuan, pounds or euros. Altcoins helped remove some of the significant barriers to investing in bitcoin, by allowing people with small-scale hardware to mine altcoins and trade them for bitcoins. Via the proliferating exchanges, the altcoin boom strengthened the price of bitcoin, as it became the 'anchor currency' of the cryptocurrency economy.

Does cryptocurrency have a future?

Much of the debate on this issue is linked to the fate of the original cryptocurrency: bitcoin. Even the developers working on bitcoin software feel this anxiety. A number have quit publicly, after personal disagreements with other bitcoin proponents. Everyone can agree that bitcoin is facing serious challenges. It seems no one can agree on what to do about it.

Many people have invested millions of dollars into bitcoin, either directly in the currency, or as companies developing bitcoin-based products. While companies can go bankrupt and individual investors and developers can become fed-up and quit, it is highly unlikely that everyone will walk away from bitcoin, abandoning their money, and going on to something else. Bitcoin was the first cryptocurrency, and earns a significant amount of allegiance based on that fact alone. This was the cryptocurrency that Satoshi Nakamoto built. It is likely that bitcoin will be around for decades to come — but whether it will be anything like the bitcoin of today, is anyone's guess. New technical evolutions, or a stagnation in growth could cause bitcoin to either explode in the numbers of new users, or retreat to the backwaters of the internet.

12
It's not about the money

The true value of cryptocurrencies such as bitcoin may not lie in coins. Technological innovations arising from the blockchain itself could turn out to be far more exciting. So where will they lead?

In its heyday in 2013, bitcoin's value peaked at around $1,200 per coin. Not surprisingly, the cryptocurrency was feted as the 'future of money'. Today, with bitcoin's value halved, media interest has also waned. Yet all kinds of businesses, along with city investors and futurists have found something else about the technology to get excited over – in particular, the potential of the blockchain itself.

The blockchain is, of course, the central innovation that allows cryptocurrencies to function (see 'The blockchain', Chapter 4). But this shift in attention has occurred as people working with the technology have realized that the blockchain might be good for a great many things besides cryptocurrencies.

It turns out that a digital, decentralized ledger is useful for handling all kinds of information, from business contracts or private financial records to sensitive healthcare data. And people are scrambling to determine what might best be kept in the blockchain, and whether that blockchain should be attached to bitcoin, another cryptocurrency, or something completely different. Most surprisingly, this research is not just coming from tiny startups or libertarian hackers. Some of the most ambitious projects are being run by mainstream financial institutions such as major banks. They are determined to understand the true potential of this powerful technology, and not be left behind any financial revolution.

Blockchains as research tools

One criticism of bitcoin is that maintaining a large network generating hash, simply to support a cryptocurrency through the proof-of-work is a huge waste of time and electricity. For bitcoin, the proof-of-work algorithm is called SHA-256, and it is a fairly standard cryptographic algorithm. Indeed, many research tasks require computers to do similar work to hashing – crunching through enormous sets of very small problems in order to solve a task by brute force. Perhaps it was unsurprising then, that a few years after bitcoin appeared, experiments began in which SHA-256 was replaced by another algorithm specially designed to harness all that computing power for other means.

In 2013, a programmer with the pseudonym Sunny King announced a cryptocurrency called Primecoin. What distinguishes it from bitcoin was that it harnessed the proof-of-work in order to discover new members of a class of prime numbers called Cunningham chains. These are not the largest prime numbers, which require massive supercomputers to discover and prove, but sets of prime numbers where by taking one prime, doubling it and subtracting one, another prime number is given, and so on. Though Primecoin was never particularly popular as a currency, its proof-of-work has revealed some record-breaking Cunningham chains.

Another cryptocurrency, Riecoin, set out to solve another set of problems involving prime numbers. The proof-of-work, in this case, is looking for clusters of consecutive primes called 'constellations'. These prime constellations could potentially be used to aid work on the Riemann hypothesis. The Riemann hypothesis is a complicated mathematics question that has yet to be proven, remaining one outstanding mystery of the field. It is so well known, it has been designated one of the seven Millennium Prize Problems by the Clay Mathematics Institute. Named in 2000, thus far only one has been solved, despite a reward prize of $1 million for a successful proof. The prime constellations would not prove the Riemann hypothesis, but they could potentially discover a prime constellation that would disprove the hypothesis – a discovery of great theoretical importance in its own right. Most mathematicians expect that the Riemann hypothesis will eventually be shown to hold true, but in the meantime, Riecoin is working on testing it.

A new address book for the internet

While the blockchain could help with the discovery of new prime number combinations, it has also been trialled as a practical way to help keep internet records safe. The code for each website on the internet is stored on a particular computer server, with the website's name linked to the unique address – or 'IP address' – of this server through the domain name system (DNS). Surprisingly, perhaps, for a global system, the DNS records for the entire world are held in databases stored in just 13 servers.

In 2011, it was suggested that DNS records could be decentralized by putting them in the blocks of a blockchain associated with a new currency called Namecoin, a relative of bitcoin. Just as transaction records of other cryptocurrencies are stored in the blockchain, the Namecoin blockchain was able to store the DNS records for websites using a .bit top level domain designator.

Yet while Namecoin worked fine, it never caught on. One issue was that you needed a browser with a special add-on program to access .bit sites via the Namecoin DNS information. Also, most websites continued to use the standard DNS registry. Very few legitimate websites ever registered in the Namecoin blockchain. In fact, of the 196,000 sites in the Namecoin registry, it was estimated that the vast majority did not even have a website attached to the name. In May 2016, the last major exchange trading Namecoin stopped dealing with the cryptocurrency, and the experiment ended.

BOINC

Others have pursued more ambitious uses for the blockchain. Back in 2002, a team based at the spce sciences lab at the University of California, Berkeley, developed software called the Berkeley Open Infrastructure for Network Computing, or BOINC. Their idea was to harness the power of computers around the world to help a group of researchers at the Search for Extraterrestrial Intelligence (SETI) Institute sift through radio signals from space to hunt for signs of aliens.

BOINC allowed them to spread the effort of this search task by chopping up signals into small batches and sending them out to individual computers which, when sitting unused, would look for signs of alien communication. Once a computer had completed one batch, the results were returned to SETI and new batches received. The trick was that the search program behaved like a screensaver, only running at night or when the computer was idle. Named the SETI@HOME project, it rapidly became one of the largest distributed computing efforts in the world. And today BOINC doesn't just look for aliens – the software is now used to hunt for new cures for diseases, to map the Milky Way, and even to crack codes.

Replacing proof-of-work with proof-of-stake

In 2015, a researcher named Rob Halford wondered if he could connect BOINC to a cryptocurrency. BOINC was already set up to divide computer tasks amongst many computers. In addition, it could call on large numbers of people willing to run its software. If those individuals were rewarded with cryptocurrency for their efforts, and if existing currency miners could also be drawn into using BOINC, everyone could benefit. But in order to do that, the researchers would have to utilize an entirely new sort of blockchain that would free up computers from the necessity of creating proof-of-work hash. While proof-of-work was necessary to the functioning of the blockchain of cryptocurrencies like bitcoin, it severely limited the sort of otherwise useful tasks that a cryptocurrency mining could complete. To scale the difficulty properly (see 'Proof-of-work', Chapter 4) the proof-of-work task has to be very specific. When downloading new files from the central server for processing, BOINC often has the computer work on different sorts of tasks, and doing the same task over and over would not necessarily be productive, outside of very particular tasks like looking for prime numbers. But if proof-of-work was not required to secure the blockchain transaction logging, then that processing power would be available to perform more useful tasks, like BOINC calculations.

The first cryptocurrency to show that it was possible to move away from proof-of-work was called Peercoin. It replaced proof-of-work with a method called '**proof-of-stake**'. This proof-of-stake creates a value for each coin in the cryptocurrency, called 'coin age'. The longer a coin had been held without being spent, the 'older' it is. Every time it is spent, it is 'reborn', and its age resets to zero.

When it was time to create the next block, the Peercoin network would decide that the block was to be created by the computer in the network with the wallet with the most coin age – that is, the person who had owned the most coins without spending them, the longest. It is possible to predict which wallet has the highest coin age, so this process is not random. But nevertheless, it is secure: after the block is created, the coin age of that computer's coins are reset to zero. Therefore, a computer can never form a block twice in a row. In order to mess with the blockchain by double-spending, two computers would have to save up a tremendous amount of wealth in the cryptocurrency in order to guarantee it the chance to create a block, not just once, but twice in a row, in order to create contradicting transactions. As the coin age is reset, there would be no way for someone to reuse that coin age to promote a usurper blockchain with false transactions. It is theorized that anyone with that amount of wealth wouldn't risk damaging the blockchain, because the amount of investment they would lose from a price crash in the aftermath of a successful attack would pale in comparison to how much they might make with a faulty transaction.

Most important of all, proof-of-stake eliminates the proof-of-work role for the blockchain, making it less demanding on computer processors. The coin age is the only thing necessary to trigger a new block, no computer-intensive hashing is required. Using a hybrid of proof-of-stake with the valuable computing work done by BOINC, Rob Halford's new cryptocurrency Gridcoin rewarded BOINC users with coins for contributing to any project in the BOINC network.

Wait, what happened to proof-of-work?

In the entire (albeit short) history of cryptocurrency, proof-of-work has been the fundamental activity in securing the blockchain. Thousands of mining computers churn through electricity, creating randomized cryptographic hash, without which bitcoin could not function. So what happened to turn this state of affairs upside down? How did proof-of-work suddenly become unnecessary?

The thinking behind bitcoin and proof-of-work cryptocurrencies is that all computers on the network are equal, and all computers are equally likely to attempt to take over the blockchain by issuing bad transactions or by changing transactions that already exist. From the amount of value in the system, one might conclude that an attempt to defect against the network would be highly likely. Proof-of-work makes it so incredibly hard for any computer to take over the network, this hypothesized mass defection becomes nearly impossible. Hashing is a hard limit that affects each computer equally, and increases in effectiveness the more computers take part. It is like a fence around a herd of sheep, that grows in size and height the more sheep are added to the flock.

But beginning with proof-of-stake, a new paradigm began to grow. In this thinking, the most important nodes are those with a lot of stake in the system. Each of these nodes has a great deal of investment in the network, and a situation in which multiple nodes could be controlled by the same attacker is very unlikely. It this case, it is in the nodes' interest to agree, rather than defect. Therefore, consensus is assumed to be likely, and the primary task is to catch wayward nodes and get them back on track. To use the analogy of sheep again, the herd's tendency is to stay together, and all that is required is a sheepdog to find the lost sheep and chase them back to the herd.

So if proof-of-work is not necessary, why is it still in use? Bitcoin's users are more conservative and suspicious of big changes, perhaps. But even new blockchains like Ethereum still use proof-of-work (see 'The age of Ethereum', Chapter 13). The reasons are varied. Some cryptocurrency designers still want mining to exist, as an impetus for users to join the network and support the cryptocurrency. Others want the nodes to be more democratic, unlike blockchains that privilege particular nodes with a greater stake. Additionally, some don't yet trust the proof-of-stake concept, and feel that proof-of-work is more tested – after all, if it works for bitcoin, it must be good. Right now, there are proponents for each method. But in the future, we might see a strong preference for one over the other across the many blockchain applications that are currently in development.

Banks and blockchains

As cryptocurrencies have become more valuable, and the usefulness of blockchains to collect and store accounting information has become apparent, the blockchain has begun to look less like a marginal experiment. Economists, bankers, as well as blockchain proponents, have all started to examine how blockchains might function within existing financial markets, not as an alternatives to them.

For instance, large banks such as Santander, Barclays, and Citi-Bank are rushing to study and invest in blockchain technology – not just to use as a mechanism for digital currencies, but as a ledger, pure and simple. Using a decentralized, secure ledger could allow investors to secure ownership records in small companies that can change hands often and which have very specific rules about voting rights and shareholder agreements. The Nasdaq, the second-largest stock market exchange in the world, is partnering with blockchain startup Chain to build a blockchain to secure records for their private market platform, to allow registration and trading of non-publicly traded companies. And one US company, Overstock.com, recently received approval from the US Securities and Exchange Commission to issue stock using a blockchain-based bond system called TØ.

The blockchain could make banks as we know them a thing of the past.

Another company, Factom, is working on a way to create a time-stamped blockchain ledger that can be used by any company. This blockchain wouldn't be publicly accessible, rather only available for employees and branches within a company, and used for sharing records across the business. The Singapore Central Bank is also interested in this sort of blockchain, and began funding the development of their own blockchain-based record keeping system in 2015.

Spanish bank Santander released a report in 2015 praising the ability of blockchains to handle contracts between different parties of a supply chain. Rather than interfacing between the different accounting systems of wholesalers and shipping companies, a single blockchain could track materials and product shipments between any number of companies.

Yet so far there is no consensus over exactly what the most useful blockchain technology application might be. At least two large consortiums of banks and businesses have been organized to promote blockchain technology in its most general form, hoping that the specific applications are worked out later. The Post-Trade Distributed Ledger (PTDL) Group counts HSBC, The London Stock Exchange, and Société Générale among its members. The other consortium, called R3, includes Goldman Sachs, JP Morgan, Deutsche Bank, the Royal Bank of Canada, and many more banks from around the world. Neither consortium has announced details of technologies they are developing, and are only in the most basic organizational stages.

Meanwhile, software developers and technologists are not being left out. W3C, the main international standards organization for the internet, has been leading discussions on what role the blockchain might have in the technology underlying the internet. And the Linux Foundation is running the Hyperledger Project, with the goal of developing an open-source blockchain-based ledger capable of being adapted to all sorts of uses – an equivalent to Linux, its open-source operating system.

How to transfer money around the world

Every bank that does business in a particular country must have an account with the country's central bank. Using what is called a **'real-time gross settlement'** (RTGS) system run by a subsidiary of the central bank, banks may send each other funds back and forth, which are then credited and debited to their accounts at the central bank. In essence, banks all become customers at a larger bank,

and handle transactions for their customers by requesting transfers at the bank where they themselves are a
'customer'.

There are some RTGS systems that cross national
borders, but eventually a situation happens in which a
bank's customer wants to transfer funds to a bank outside
of the RTGS system. To complete these transfers, banks
rely on a much more ad hoc system of 'correspondent
accounts'. One bank literally creates its own account
with another bank, and vice versa. When customers want
to transfer funds across the two banks, the two banks
must communicate the amount, agree on an exchange
rate, and then make the according changes to their own
correspondent accounts. The two banks must trust each
other to conduct these transactions – not a difficult task
in the world of banking business when billions must be
transferred back and forth each day – but it still requires
a contractual system to be set up between every two
banks that wish to conduct business this way. Occasion-
ally, banks have to form a network, using another bank
or two as an intermediary if the origin and destination banks do not already have correspondent accounts.
And there is always the time factor. Although there is an
international **SWIFT** messaging system to allow banks
to communicate these transactions, often banks are not
open at the same time due to different time zones, and
lingering transactions can conflict with changing currency exchange rates. And at some point, banks must
settle up their correspondent accounts, if they do not
otherwise balance out between institutions. Many times
this requires something as awkward or dangerous as

internationally shipping gold, cash, or other financial instruments.

Most customers transferring small amounts internationally, such as foreign workers sending money to families back home, use a transfer service like Western Union or MoneyGram, that transfers money between its offices worldwide, and then balances its accounts on the back end, using international bank transfers. But these services often charge a fee of as much as 10 per cent or more to the customer.

New blockchain technologies like Ripple could have the capacity to change the way money is sent around the world – not just for the large banks, but for everyday customers as well, utilizing new services working off a radical new financial technology backbone, called the blockchain.

A blockchain for anything

In Dubai there is an innovative new building called the Museum of the Future. Its purpose is to show off new technologies that could radically change the way lives play out around the globe. Yet experimentation is also one of its most important roles. To this end, the museum has created the Global Blockchain Council (GBC), a consortium of companies working on blockchain technology, that is developing pilot projects to bring it into unexplored areas.

Financial transactions are only the start. The GBC is also testing the blockchain to secure medical records, to provide a chain of custody information for diamonds to prevent profit from 'conflict diamonds', for transferring property records and digital wills, and even as a way to offer tourists coupons and incentives.

The Museum of the Future is not alone in such exploration. Companies and governments around the world have been announcing their own technology projects. For example, the UK government is running a six-month trial to use the blockchain to manage benefits payments. The payments are made in pounds sterling, but the transactions are logged in a digital ledger. The government of Estonia is collaborating with a company called Guardtime to build a blockchain of citizens' health records, and with another company, Bitnation, to provide a blockchain-based digital notary service. Authorities in the Republic of Georgia are building a similar system with the company BitFury, a bitcoin mining business, to manage land titles. In Sweden, the government is also testing the possibility of a blockchain-based land registry in partnership with a company called ChromaWay.

Other interesting collaborations might bear unexpected fruit. Bosch, the German-based engineering company, is working with the ASIC-makers 21 Inc. to explore the future for ASIC chips in Bosch's distributed sensor arrays. The idea is to combine microelectromechanical sensors, connected via the internet, with small computers the size of credit cards capable of mining bitcoins and processing cryptocurrency transactions. By connecting these technologies together, it could be feasible to create a global network of sensors organized through a blockchain which can offer its data to anyone who needs it, and be paid for this service in cryptocurrency. A proof-of-concept is 21 Inc.'s Ping21 service. Web hosts must measure the speed of internet traffic running through the network to check it is working. To do this they send out test messages, or pings. But rather than using dedicated computers around the world for this task, Ping21 allows any participating 21 Inc. computer to do the job and be paid for it.

Other companies are also attempting to see if they can harness the blockchain to help with real world services. Online letting agency Airbnb recently began experiments to use a blockchain as a way to manage user reputations. The company relies on reviews left by both renters and landlords so that customers can judge how trustworthy potential hosts or guests will be. Storing this information in a decentralized blockchain not only frees up Airbnb's servers, but the data could potentially be rented out to other companies using similar business models.

A blockchain could even help solve a problem for music artists and distributors. A startup called Ujo is trying to use the Ethereum blockchain to transform the music industry payment system. The aim is to allow musicians and distributors to share details of rights and royalties for music tracks online, all within smart contracts that automatically license recordings and which take payment each time they are played.

Blockchain technology could also help make digital content more widely available, not just easier to control. ZeroNet is an attempt to create not just a decentralized DNS system, but an entirely decentralized internet. It aims to side-step the need to host websites on servers by stashing website information across the internet in small pieces, which can be linked together using a blockchain-like registry. This eliminates web hosting costs, and since it integrates a bitcoin payment system, users can send payments directly to websites, as the site address doubles as a bitcoin address.

The Interplanetary File System (IPFS) is another attempt to create a distributed internet. Using a similar system to a blockchain, IPFS creates an address for every piece of content on the system – everything from images, to media files, to text. These addresses can be updated by the person who added them to the system, updating content as necessary using cryptographic keys. The content itself is then stored across multiple computers rather than on a single server. While IPFS is not attempting to create the same integration with cryptocurrency as ZeroNet, it manages the content more efficiently by using its blockchain-like structure to only store the links to the content, not the content itself. This saves space and time.

Of course, the vast majority of these ideas are in the proof-of-concept stage. And as failures and flaws continue to emerge in cryptocurrency and the blockchain, many of these ideas will sink from sight. Yet it could take just one of these schemes to succeed and we could all be using blockchain technology everyday.

Blockchain grid to let neighbours trade solar power

Something odd is happening on President Street in Brooklyn. While solar panels on the roofs of terraced houses soak up sun, a pair of computers connected to the panels quietly crunch numbers. First, they count how many electrons are being generated. Then, they write that number to a blockchain. Welcome to the future of energy exchange.

This project, run by a startup called Transactive Grid, is the first version of a new kind of energy market, operated by consumers, which will change the way we generate and consume electricity. Transactive Grid aims to enable people to buy and sell renewable energy to their neighbours. To deal in energy at the moment, you have to go through a central company like Duke Energy in the US or National Grid in the UK, or one of their resellers.

Transactive can skip this central authority because its energy market is built on blockchain technology to create a cryptographically secure list of transactions which is continuously updated as each transaction is completed. The list for President Street deals with buying and selling electrons generated by solar panels. No central authority is in control: the computers monitor each other to stop fraud.

The technology behind bitcoin is enabling a
new solar power network.

The first devices were installed on President Street in February 2016. Other companies are hot on Transactive's heels. Grid Singularity, based in Vienna, Austria, wants to bring the same decentralized energy market to developing countries, to help distribute solar power.

MIT start-up SolarCoin pays people with an alternative digital currency for generating solar energy, one coin for 1 megawatt-hour of solar electricity. And in August 2016, a groups of neighbours in Busselton, Western Australia, began testing a system to trade excess energy from solar panels between themselves using a blockchain to record the transactions.

Article by Aviva Rutkin for New Scientist *magazine.*

13
From bitcoin to autonomous corporations

Alternatives forms of the blockchain are springing up, and could revolutionize the way corporations work.

The proof-of-work blockchain used by bitcoin and other first-generation cryptocurrencies can be slow, and requires lots of computing power. Taking proof-of-stake as a starting point for potential alternatives, some blockchain developers have gone back to the drawing board to hunt for the easiest ways to achieve a consensus in which a majority of computers on a network agrees on the true state of the blockchain, in as little time as possible.

One route has been to introduce different tiers to a cryptocurrency network. Rather than a single, network of computers, this uses '**intermediate nodes**' to create two separate, but linked, networks – one for general users, and one for trusted computers forming the backbone of the network.

One of the first currencies to use this idea is Dash (originally launched as XCoin). It works by breaking the network up into two classes – the proof-of-work mining network, which anyone can join, and the 'masternode' network. In order to become a masternode, a computer must invest or lock away 1000 units of the cryptocurrency. At this point the only thing that this computer will do is function as part of the verifying service for the currency. The miners create blocks by proof-of-work just as with bitcoin, but the **masternodes** are responsible for approving each block amongst themselves using a consensus procedure. Block rewards are split between the two networks.

Many of the vulnerabilities of a standard proof-of-work cryptocurrency are avoided by using a second, verifying network operating outside the block creator network. For example, the 51% Attack, in which a miner producing 51% of the hash of a proof-of-work cryptocurrency could alter the blockchain (see 'Strength in numbers', Chapter 5), cannot occur, because the masternodes would not approve a new, falsified blockchain. Taking control of 51% of the hashrate would not allow an attacker to usurp the authority of the masternodes, and taking control of 51% of the masternodes would require a nearly insurmountable amount of currency to be stockpiled to enable the attack. The intermediate node system also allows faster transaction confirmation, because masternode consensus occurs while blocks are being mined, rather than once the block is solved. By the time the block is solved, all the masternodes have confirmed the transactions beyond any doubt.

Proof-of-work calculations might not be needed for the blockchains of the future.

Working by consensus

Dash's consensus-based approach has triggered huge interest among those developing the next wave of blockchain systems. With it has come the realization that the fundamental role of a blockchain is to agree on something, and to reach this agreement as quickly as possible (see 'Proof-of-work', Chapter 4). Once someone has unlocked their wallet and created a transaction, the primary task of the blockchain is to record that transaction, and to do this as quickly as possible so the transaction cannot be reversed, and so new transactions can be added.

A company called Ripple has developed perhaps the largest, most evolved sort of consensus blockchain yet. Its software, also named Ripple, is based on a new form of blockchain designed to handle inter-bank transfers across national borders, and even across different national currencies.

By using a maths and computer science experiment known as the '**Byzantine Generals problem**', the Ripple engineers believe they have shown that both proof-of-work and proof-of-stake are unnecessary (See box 'How does Ripple work?', below). Ripple's blockchain ledger is designed not only to facilitate transfers of the blockchain's own native currency, called XRP, but transactions in any currency. In a sense, the Ripple blockchain forms its own secure correspondent account system (see box 'How to transfer money around the world', Chapter 12), allowing any bank to create transactions between any other.

After being set up with the hardware by Ripple, a bank becomes a node in the Ripple network. Rather than communicating using a conventional currency exchange system to debit or credit accounts, two banks can exchange transaction information in the ledger, using any currency they prefer. The changes are shown on the ledger in real time. And, if a currency exchange is necessary, the network will automatically find the best price for the transaction using intermediary 'market makers' holding reserves of multiple currencies and then update all accounts. XRP can even be used to facilitate the transaction, without the nodes at either end even knowing that a cryptocurrency is involved. These transactions are settled in about one minute, no matter where they are taking place.

By relying on a system of consensus among trusted nodes, the Ripple network allows worldwide transactions between participating banks with almost no overhead costs other than the price of currency exchange. The company hopes that it will cut down on the fees associated with international money exchange. However, only banks and companies can be nodes in the Ripple network. Ordinary customers must open up an account with one of these banks, and that company uses Ripple to send the money to another bank for them. This allows the bank to continue to set the price for the transaction. In this way, Ripple hopes to put blockchain ledger technology in the mainstream by marketing to those who already control the system, rather than disrupting the money transfer industry. As of February 2017, Ripple's XRP cryptocurrency is the third-largest cryptocurrency in total value, after bitcoin and Ethereum.

How does Ripple work?

The Byzantine Generals problem imagines a number of generals, each with their own army, surrounding an enemy city. Each general is cut off from the others by hills that make it impossible for them to signal directly to each other. The strength of the enemy city is such that if all the generals attack at once they will defeat it, but if all generals but one attack, they will be repelled. The generals have to plan the time of attack by exchanging messages. However, it is impossible to guarantee the authenticity of the messages coming in – one or more of the generals is secretly on the side of the city, and sends messages to deceive the rest. So, what do the generals do?

It turns out that if less than 66 per cent of the generals are loyal, there is no way to coordinate a successful attack. However, if more than 66 per cent of the generals are loyal, then they can trust the majority of the messages they receive in order to coordinate their attack successfully. This result was proved by researchers at Microsoft in 1982. And it is exactly this fact that Ripple employs to secure its blockchain.

The Ripple blockchain network is formed from a limited number of intermediary nodes. These verify all additions to the blockchain, and communicate with the wider user base, not unlike the masternodes of Dash. All intermediary nodes communicate with each other to share transaction information, submitted by general users. However, when it is time to write a new block to the chain, they refer to a 'Unique Node List' of specific nodes that they trust. Each of these intermediary nodes creates their own list, from other intermediary nodes that they specifically trust, and believe will not attempt to defraud the blockchain. Then, the nodes compare their transactions with their list. If the transaction is agreed on by 80 per cent of the list, then it is considered included in the block consensus, and joins the blockchain. If it does not meet that 80 per cent threshold, then the transaction is carried over to the next block.

Ripple only allows particular users to join the group of intermediary nodes based on how trustworthy the network believes the users to be. As long as more than

66 per cent of its nodes are honest, the Byzantine Generals problem shows that security of the blockchain is assured. But Ripple goes a step further, by asking the nodes to poll only their trusted nodes. And just to be extra careful, Ripple requires an 80 per cent agreement level. If any transaction can't reach consensus in this way, it is held over. In this way, the blockchain allows transactions with obvious consensus to proceed as quickly as possible, while flagging confusing transactions and making them wait for agreement.

Smart contracts

Many of the recent innovations involving the blockchain focus on the concept of including additional information along with or instead of cryptocurrency transactions in the ledger. Ripple allows records of other currency transactions, Nxt allows additional text to enable the sorting of different groups or categories of cryptocurrency (called 'colours') which could allow different kinds of assets like property or commodities to be represented on the blockchain. Companies like Chain and Factom are figuring out how to log ownership and shareholder information in the blockchain. Software updates have even been proposed for bitcoin's blockchain that would increase the size of the block to allow more transactions. These might bring additional text or cryptographic facilities to the blockchain that would deliver entirely new features.

Some of the greatest excitement in the world of blockchain development involves putting not just transactions or data in the blockchain, but code itself. This would allow the blockchain to act as a decentralized program, in effect running software that could update and alter itself in response to changing conditions in the market. This code could enable what are known as 'smart contracts' that function autonomously. However, researchers are discovering that this new realm of combined code and legalese is giving birth to serious complexities.

Smart contracts were first suggested by virtual currency developer Nick Szabo in 1997. The idea is fairly straightforward: when buying a house, for example, the money and deeds are usually passed to a trusted third-party such as a lawyer or a bank. When the third-party is satisfied that both sides of the deal have fulfilled their contract requirements, they hand over the money and the deeds, accordingly. A smart contract could do this automatically, without requiring a third-party. Both deeds and money are given to the program in digital form, along with the terms of the agreement. When the smart contract observes that the terms are fulfilled, it delivers the digital payment and product directly. The blockchain secures the code of the contract in the decentralized mechanism of the ledger, in the same way that it secures the transactions of a cryptocurrency. The same blockchain might hold the deed, the payment, and the contract, simply updating its ledger to account for the new, swapped ownership.

Such contracts don't have to be large or complex. For example, something as simple as a parking meter could run code in a blockchain – when the parking payment is received, it registers the vehicle as legally parked. A smart contract could simply be a voting mechanism. Rather than receiving any money, the code could accept votes from registered shareholders and report the final tally. And there are also contracts in which the blockchain code doesn't have to make any decisions whatsoever, but instead could behave like a digital storage locker. Money goes into the locker, and cannot be removed until both parties agree to open the locker, using their public-encryption key. Some of these simple contract ideas could be deployed in future versions of bitcoin, like the proposed Lightning Network (see 'The Lightning Network', Chapter 11).

The age of Ethereum

Now that smart contracts have captured the attention of blockchain developers, other possibilities are starting to emerge. Could blockchains manage shareholder voting mechanisms, for instance? Could they even control entire corporations?

From a legal perspective, a corporation is no more than a series of rules defining leadership, ownership, and profit-sharing structures. Perhaps something like this really could be written into code, and then secured in the blockchain. This could be described as an 'autonomous corporation'.

In 2015, a Russian programmer called **Vitalik Buterin** launched Ethereum, a blockchain that allows smart contracts to be embedded within it. Using a custom programming language called Solidity, programmers can upload their code to the Ethereum blockchain, paying a small fee in Ether, the blockchain's cryptocurrency. Once the code is implanted into a block, it receives an address. Anyone may then target the address using their computer, and run the code contained inside. The limits of what the code can do are up to the programmer. It might be a small program that responds with generic text, or a simple contract that only responds to specific people with authorization. In theory, it could also be an autonomous corporation programmed to buy something useful, rent it out, and then take payment – all within the distributed Ethereum blockchain.

The potential of Ethereum has led to a renaissance in the idealism that gave birth to bitcoin, and autonomous corporations have become the new dream for libertarian proponents of cryptography. If an entire business can be held in a distributed, decentralized blockchain beyond the jurisdiction of any nation, it offers an entirely new notion of 'free'. Who would collect taxes from an autonomous corporation? To which politicians would a blockchain-based business have to bow? Imperfections of governments could be side-stepped, replaced by code – simple, open-source and accessible to anyone with programming skills, yet ultimately secure and free from human weakness. Investors infected by this idealism leapt at the chance to support Ethereum, and Ether became the second-largest cryptocurrency after bitcoin.

All kinds of proposals began to appear in the wake of Ethereum's launch. For instance, a Swiss company named Slock.it came up with a plan to build a lock – the physical kind, that fits on a door – that could connect to the internet and the Ethereum blockchain. This would allow people to use the blockchain to rent property, for a short time such as a holiday period, and the lock would only open the door when the customer had paid the fee, and lock automatically again when the rental period was over.

Ripple versus Ethereum

One way of looking at the future of the blockchain is as a contest between Ripple and Ethereum. Ethereum embodies much of the idealistic spirit of the early days of cryptocurrencies. It was this spirit that brought about the DAO (see below), and was also the means of its collapse. In the rush to make something new, mistakes are often made. Ripple, on the other hand, seems to embrace a more conventional approach. Rather than attempting to forge new ground, Ripple is appealing to those already in control of the financial networks. Rather than a revolution, it is offering a product. And indeed, Ripple has toned

---

down some of its early aspirations in order to better target a service it thinks that banks might buy.

Which is the right way of doing things? Both are trying new ideas with completely new markets, and so far no clear winner has emerged.

Yet this could provide a useful perspective by helping us categorize new financial technologies. Is a technology 'with the system' or 'against it', idealistic or realistic, revolutionary or incrementalist? Is it out to prove new concepts, or just out to make a buck? These questions might help us understand the motivations of the developers and proponents of the technology. Judging the technology itself, however, will require different criteria, and eventual success is far harder to predict.

Autonomous corporations

The Decentralized Autonomous Organization (DAO) was born when Christoph Jentzch, brother of Slock.it CEO Simon Jentzch, had an ambitious plan. He decided to try to create the sort of autonomous corporation that Ethereum creator Vitalik Buterin had first discussed. So he began writing code, and with support from Slock.it, published it to the Ethereum blockchain in early 2016.

The idea behind the DAO seems relatively simple. The DAO would be a vehicle for crowdfunding. Potential funders would buy shares in the DAO, called DAO Tokens, using Ether, the native Ethereum cryptocurrency. These tokens granted voting rights in proportion to the number purchased. From these sales, the DAO accumulated cryptocurrency capital which it was then able to invest.

Next, people would submit suggestions for services to the DAO, attempting to win funding from the DAO's stockpile of capital. They might suggest doing a task, for example, like editing code for the DAO, or building and selling some sort of Ethereum-based product, or even do charity work. Those offering services, called 'contractors', would also suggest how much they should be paid for them, or whether they would give some profits from their scheme to the DAO. The Token holders in the DAO would then vote on the proposal. If it was approved, the contractor would do the work, and when the terms of their contract were fulfilled, the DAO would pay them. If any profit came back to the DAO, it would be shared between the Token holders.

The DAO idea became wildly popular, raising over $150 million in Ether – the most successful crowd funding project in history. But soon, complications with the DAO's programming began to emerge.

The boardroom of the future?

It turned out that the DAO was susceptible to its own sort of 51% Attack (see 'Proof-of-work, Chapter 4). If one person managed to get 51% of the DAO Tokens, they could automatically control any vote that took place. The attacker could submit a proposal that said, in essence, 'give me all of the DAO's money', and then it would provide the majority vote to approve the plan.

To prevent this a number of defence protocols were created. First, a role of 'curator' was added. Held by a real person, the job was to personally approve every outbound payment. Second, it was decided that important votes (anything more than a straw poll) would be conducted in two parts. The first would be a vote on the question at hand, either to approve or deny the proposal. Then, the vote would come back to the Token holders again, giving them the choice to either accept the outcome of the first vote, or choose to split. If they accepted the outcome (whether they voted yes or no), they would remain in the DAO. If they chose to split, their Tokens and accompanying voting rights would be transferred to a **'Child DAO'**, exactly like the original DAO in every way, but separate. In other words, the split function gave the shareholders the opportunity to secede from the DAO if they ever disagreed with a vote.

Almost immediately, complications emerged. First, among a number of different proposals put to the Token holders of the DAO in the first few weeks of its existence, not a single one was able to achieve a quorum. The quorum was determined algorithmically, but at a minimum it needed to be 20 per cent of the Token holders. Yet most proposals garnered just 10 per cent voting at most. Some blamed this on technical difficulties with voting. Others thought that many Token holders had bought them as an investment, and weren't interested in the principles of the DAO or in participating in its management. Indeed, the price of the Tokens had skyrocketed as Tokens had been sold, but few were taking part in the day-to-day discussions about the future of the DAO.

But a second, more serious problem emerged. A number of programmers thought they had found a vulnerability in the DAO code, which allowed a Token holder to withdraw their own money and pull out of the DAO. It meant a user could trick the DAO by asking for withdrawals multiple times, during which the DAO would only check the user's account balance once. This attack was not unlike the transaction malleability problem (see 'What is the transaction malleability problem?', Chapter 4) in that by exploiting the bug, an attacker could withdraw double the amount of money they actually had in their account. (Although from a code standpoint, the two problems were not at all alike.) By performing this **recursive split attack** many successive times, a criminal could easily drain the DAO of its cryptocurrency.

A week after the vulnerability was announced, an attacker struck. Nearly \$80 million worth of Ether, around a third of the DAO's total holdings, was withdrawn. Those holding DAO Tokens, as well as the larger Ethereum community, panicked, and the value of Tokens and Ether crashed on cryptocurrency exchanges.

Saving the DAO

An immediate and obvious solution was a hard fork of the Ethereum blockchain. Because the code for the DAO was within the blockchain, it could not just be rolled back to reverse the theft. The same blockchain that preserved the DAO also made the DAO difficult to alter or update. However, if the entirety of the blockchain was rolled back, all the money could be refunded to the original investors, and it would be as if the theft had never occurred.

This solution was ethically troubling for many. A founding idea of Ethereum was that code defined existence in the blockchain. If the blockchain could be forked any time there was a mistake, what did that mean for the code's supposed 'immutability'? Even those who had lost money in the theft didn't like the implications. Then, compounding the dispute, someone claiming to be the attacker published a blog post in which they criticized the founders of the DAO for their backpedalling. The DAO, the attacker claimed, was created to replace law with code, warts and all. The attacker hadn't stolen anything, in their own view. They had merely found a legal loophole. They had merely played by the inimically broken rules of the 'immutable, unstoppable, and irrefutable computer code' as lionized by the DAO's founders, and so they demanded their reward. If others suffered losses, that was only their own fault for not scrutinizing the code.

Taunting aside, it turned out that the attacker hadn't got clean away with the money. The nature of the recursive split attack meant that the attacker couldn't just leave with the stolen funds, but had to 'split out' using the Child DAO functionality. And in using the split function, a waiting period of 27 days was triggered, per the original code (meant to give the person splitting into a Child DAO a grace period to consider their options).

Programmers tracking the theft discovered the Child DAO into which the attacker had withdrawn the stolen funds; it was simply a forgotten split proposal that had been left open. The programmers, collectively calling themselves 'Robin Hood', then performed the *same* recursive split attack on the stolen funds, withdrawing them into yet another Child DAO, one step down the line. But again, they would be locked into a 27-day waiting period, during which time the original attacker could strike again.

But this endless limbo did suggest another options: a soft fork. In this case, the vulnerability could be closed, and if everything was timed right, eventually all the funds that were in the hands of Robin Hood and other benevolent attackers could likely be returned to their original owners, although the process was complex and not sure to work. The benefit of this solution was that the Ethereum blockchain would not need to be permanently changed.

But in the end, all the developers began to agree that the soft fork was a gamble. There might be other vulnerabilities in the process that were yet undiscovered. The hard fork was really the best option. It would also close the DAO permanently, and return all Ether to those who had originally purchased DAO Tokens.

On 20 July 2016, the hard fork was rolled out. Users of the Ethereum blockchain could choose to run the new, forked version of the software, or carry on using the old version. The vast majority, over 85 per cent, chose the new fork. All the funds from the DAO, now funnelled into that fork, are being returned to their original owners.

But a significant number of Ethereum users did not adopt the fork, and in essence, split the Ethereum blockchain. As of August 2016, there are now two Ethereum blockchains, and two Ether cryptocurrencies. The one that adopted the fork is known as Ethereum One, and the blockchain that rejected the fork is called Ethereum Classic. The impact of two separate Ethereum blockchains on the DAO is not yet clear.

Lessons learned

Since the DAO funds were stolen, there have been numerous editorials on lessons to be learned. Some say events prove that real-world laws and courts are necessary to adjudicate these sorts of disputes. Others say that this episode actually proves the code works – after all, the hard fork did return Ether to all the DAO investors. Still others predict that legal authorities in Switzerland (where Ethereum, Slock.it, and the other founding companies are based) may still become involved. Meanwhile others blame it all on a failure with the Ethereum code itself, and suggest it needs to be changed.

Blockchain technology is not simple, even though it is often explained as if it is. Many stories have been told about crypto-currency stashes being lost because of the absolute secrecy of secret keys – once a secret key is lost, the wallet is locked forever. Failure after failure of exchanges, companies, and blockchains themselves show that there are still many mistakes to be made, and people capable of making them.

But one of the critical failures of the DAO was to assume that it would really be just that simple. Even setting aside the recursive split vulnerability, it is difficult to believe that anyone thought an organization allowing rampant secession upon disagreement would work. Human beings are likely to disagree, to attempt to take advantage of each other, and to try and use power structures for their own ends. It seems that the recursive split vulnerability might have saved everyone a lot of trouble by stopping the DAO before it got started, and before it fractured itself into a thousand different Child DAOs that could not come to any sort of agreement with one another.

To see just how poorly the DAO estimated human nature, one merely has to study the so-called 'Stalker Attack'. The Stalker Attack was merely hypothetical, because the DAO did not exist long enough for an instance of this abuse to ever truly occur.

The Stalker Attack was hypothesized as a situation in which a person attempts to split into a Child DAO, perhaps to withdraw their funds. Then, a 'Stalker' jumps into the Child DAO with them, bringing in enough Tokens to have a large majority over the person who initially attempted to split. In this new Child DAO, with only two people in it, the Stalker can control any vote. They can appoint themselves as Curator, and make sure that only they can receive any funds transferred out of the Child DAO. The only thing for the victim to do is to split again, into another Child DAO. Then, the Stalker follows them again, doing exactly the same thing. The victim is trapped forever, as this bully keeps controlling the vote and following the victim every time they try to split away.

According to the developers of the DAO, the Stalker Attack was a 'non-issue' because there was no motivation for the attacker to do it. The Stalker's funds would be locked up forever along with the victim's funds, as long as they continued to antagonize the victim. What possible logical motivation would anyone have to waste their own money harassing someone else?

To which, nearly anyone might answer – look at the world of politics! Look at frivolous lawsuits! Look at real-life stalkers, who spend all their time harassing someone else for no material gain! One can think of hundreds of situations in which someone with a lot of money and time would cause endless trouble for those with less money and time, either waiting for them to slip up, or otherwise give in to any number of demands so that the Stalker will let them withdraw their funds.

But the developers of the DAO, while perhaps quite well educated in the mechanics of blockchains (giving their fatal programming error the benefit of the doubt) seemed to be terribly uneducated in the mechanics of human nature. And so, whether from vulnerability, or from the hazards of overly programmatic democracy, the DAO's failure seemed inevitable.

While some might argue that it is through this sort of failure that technology evolves, the truly odd thing here is that this was not an experiment using the risk-hedged money of venture capital. Real investors expect these sorts of gambles, and are equipped to take the failure in their stride. However, with experiments like the DAO, these failures are conducted using the money of individual supporters taken from the internet. In an attempt to escape the rules and power structure of corporate capital, experiments in alternative corporations like the DAO risk everyday people's hard-earned money, asking them to believe in an unproven future with little mitigation of the risks involved. Crowdfunding experiments are presented as democratizing, allowing all to participate equally. But when it comes to the blockchain, the bottom of the economic pyramid is being used to weather the storm of mistakes, missteps, and just plain old poor judgment, so that eventually, the large banks watching from the wings can learn from these errors. A future based on this sort of experimentation does not appear as democratic, so much as using the crowd to cushion the falls of the powerful.

14

Conclusion

When *New Scientist* magazine published its special report on digital money in 2014, it seemed like a good idea to list the price of the magazine, in bitcoin, on the cover. Alas, it was not to be.

For a start, there was the issue of giving a fixed price in a currency whose value might plummet (or rocket) at any time. And how would the payments be processed? At the time, no stockists would accept bitcoin, and the situation hasn't changed much since.

That pretty much sums up where bitcoin is today, less than a decade since the idea for this radical new form of money was first mooted by 'Satoshi Nakamoto', its mysterious inventor. Interest is growing fast, but its value remains volatile, its use marginal, and its infrastructure embryonic. And you can't yet use it to buy much in the 'real' world without workarounds or contracts with special service providers – scarcely the seamless payment system you might expect, and certainly no match for the already ever present cash or cards.

Bitcoin itself may never rise to this challenge. Its foundations, so daringly different to those of traditional currencies, may be too weak to support even a small percentage of society's massive amount of financial activity. It may end up limited to an informal existence in the dark side of the internet, or co-opted by Silicon Valley and Wall Street, as previous financial innovations have been. A more outlandish scenario is that it is adopted by a desperate nation whose currency has collapsed.

But bitcoin is not the only game in town. The real innovation might be what people are doing with the core technology. The true value of the bitcoin experiment could be as a digital basis for trust: the blockchain, which allows transactions to be recorded without reams of paperwork. But dispense with the bureaucracy, and you could also displace those who make money by dealing with it.

By opening up the bitcoin protocol to the world, Satoshi Nakamoto may not have democratized finance – so much as given finance a technology as revolutionary as internet protocols. Like the internet, what originally seemed radically democratic will develop its own, new power structures. If so, it's not just the billions of dollars invested in bitcoin that are at stake, but the very nature of money itself.

Fifty ideas

This section gives you ways you can explore the subject in greater depth. It's more than just the usual reading list.

Six cryptocurrency facts

1 **Digicash.** This was the first usable virtual currency, founded in 1990. It ceased to exist just eight years later, when the company that created it folded.

2 **From spam to money.** In 1997, cryptographer Adam Back came up with an idea for reducing spam email called 'hashcash', a computing system that set hard limits on the number of emails that could be sent over a set period of time. He emailed the idea as a whitepaper to the Cypherpunks mailing list, but it was never implemented on a large scale. Bitcoin uses aspects of Back's hashcash concept.

3 **First bitcoin owner.** US computer scientist Hal Finney was the recipient of the first bitcoin transfer. He received ten coins from Nakamoto in early 2009, back when they were essentially worthless. There were also suspicions that Finney might actually be the enigmatic bitcoin founder himself.

4 **Power hungry.** Since 2011, the bitcoin network has harnessed so much processing power that it is thought to be more powerful than the top 500 supercomputers in the world combined. This means that, theoretically, even if the top 500 supercomputers were used at the same time to try and alter the bitcoin blockchain network, they could not do it.

5 **Dunning-Krugerrands.** William Gibson, author of cyberpunk novel *Neuromancer*, jokingly referred to bitcoin as 'Dunning-Krugerrands'. He derived the term from Krugerrands, a South African gold coin, and the

Dunning–Kruger Effect, a cognitive bias in which amateurs have an inflated sense of their own abilities.

6 **Bitcoin taxes.** Zug in Switzerland has become the first city in the world to accept the cryptocurrency bitcoin for government services. The pilot scheme, which started on 1 July 2016, will allow citizens to use bitcoin to pay taxes, fines and fees – as long as the amount is less than 200 Swiss francs ($205).

Seven real-world locations related to cryptocurrencies

1 **Tokyo, Japan.** Home of Mt. Gox, the now defunct bitcoin exchange.

2 **Keflavik, Iceland.** Home of the servers of Silk Road, the online dark net marketplace.

3 **Beijing, China.** Home of OKCoin, one of the largest bitcoin exchanges by volume.

4 **Hong Kong.** Home of Bitfinex, one of the largest USD/bitcoin exchanges by volume.

5 **Baar, Switzerland.** Home of Ethereum, the public blockchain-based computing platform.

6 **New York State.** Home of the BitLicense, the first financial licence specifically for cryptocurrency companies.

7 **Arnhem, The Netherlands.** One of the most 'bitcoin friendly cities', in 2016 the municipality claimed it had over 100 merchants accepting bitcoin directly for goods and services.

Six strange things bought with cryptocurrency

1 **Multi-million dollar pizza.** In April 2010, bitcoin afi-
cionado Laszlo Hanyecz convinced someone to send a
couple of pizzas to his home in exchange for 10,000
bitcoins. At the time bitcoin wasn't traded publicly, but a
few months later when Mt. Gox opened for business, the
price of one bitcoin settled at 6 cents, making Hanyecz's
pizzas cost $300 a piece (as an early miner, Hanyecz's
stash would have been quite large). At the end of 2016,
when bitcoin was trading above $700 each, those same
pizzas would be worth $3.5 million a piece.

2 **Bitcoin in space!** Virgin Galactic is not taking pas-
sengers to space just yet – but they are selling tickets.
To join the line costs $250,000. But you can pay in
bitcoins (at current exchange rate).

3 **Cryptocurrency on ice.** Because of its small value,
dogecoin was lauded as a good coin to raise money
for charity. At only a few fractions of a cent per coin,
it was easy to earn, and easy to give a few thousand
at a time to a worthy cause. Dogecoin supporters put
this claim to the test in 2014, when they raised over
$30,000 to help send the Jamaican bobsled team to the
Sochi Olympics.

4 **Crypto-whoppers.** While new bitcoin debit and credit
cards on the market might make everyday purchases
using bitcoin seem less exciting, bitcoin users were
in for a deal when the Burger King of Arnhem, The
Netherlands began accepting bitcoin directly in 2016.
Anyone buying the signature Whopper sandwich with
bitcoins received a second one free.

5 **Degree in person, paid online.** The University of Nicosia in Cyprus, Greece accepts bitcoin to pay for tuition. But, perhaps this only makes sense, given that they offer a Master of Science degree in Digital Currency.

6 **Consume at own risk.** While the online marketplace Silk Road had a reputation as a market for illegal goods, particularly drugs, the anything-goes attitude provided for some odd products on offer. Computer parts, poker lessons, designer fashion, and rare coins were all sold for bitcoins on the site. But perhaps there was nothing weirder than the offer of dried reindeer meat, direct from Finland.

Five quotes

1 'People have been defending their own privacy for centuries with whispers, darkness, envelopes, closed doors, secret handshakes, and couriers. The technologies of the past did not allow for strong privacy, but electronic technologies do.' *Eric Hughes, Cypherpunk Manifesto*

2 'What is needed is an electronic payment system based on cryptographic proof instead of trust.' *Satoshi Nakamoto*

3 'Satoshi Nakamoto is not really a man; he is a manifestation of public acclamation, an entity made by technology, and a myth.' *Andrew O'Hagan, The Satoshi Affair.*

4 'I'm reasonably confident ... that the blockchain will change a great deal of financial practice and exchange.' *Larry Summers, former US Secretary of the Treasury*

5 'Bring paper money into a country where this use of paper is unknown, and everyone will laugh at your subjective imagination.' *Karl Marx*

Five literary references

Perhaps it is no surprise that science fiction is rich source of storylines about digital money.

1 *Neuromancer* (Ace Books, 1984). William Gibsons's formative 1984 novel describes a virtual world where power is held by whoever can control the technology and where wealth moves in digital form.

2 *Cryptonomicon* (Avon Books, 1999). The 1999 novel by Neal Stephenson tells two intertwined stories – one set in the golden age of cryptography, during the Second World War, and the other in the late 1990s involving a plot of digital currencies and data havens.

3 *Reamde* (William Morrow, 2011). Another of Stephenson's novels contains a convoluted scam involving digital currency within a virtual world, but this was more like the virtual currency of a massive online role-playing game like World of Warcraft.

4 *Neptune's Brood* (Ace Books, 2013). This 2014 book by Charles Stross features a fictional universe where there are different types of money termed 'fast, medium and slow'. They involve cryptographic signatures to verify transactions, with the slower ones requiring digital signing beams by laser from a distant star (the additional time constraints make the money more secure). Stross is a widely known critic of bitcoin.

5 *Down and Out in the Magic Kingdom* (Tor Books, 2003). One of the most unique fictional explorations into virtual currency comes from writer Cory Doctorow. In this 2003 novel, he creates a currency called 'whuffle', a currency based on social reputation.

Twenty-one places to find out more

1 Bruce Sterling's *The Hacker Crackdown* (Bantam Books, 1992)

2 Steven Levy's 'Crypto Rebels'. *Wired*. May/June 1993.

3 Eric Hughes' 'Cypherpunk Manifesto'.

4 Joshuah Bearman's 'The Rise and Fall of Silk Road'. *Wired*. April 2015

5 Adam L. Penenberg's reporting for *Fast Company* and other publications.

6 Andy Greenberg's reporting for *Wired* and other publications.

7 Nathaniel Popper's *Digital Gold*, and his reporting for the *New York Times*.

8 Felix Martin's *Money: The Unauthorized Biography* (Vintage Books, 2013).

9 David Graeber's *Debt: The First 5,000 Years* (Melville House Publishing, 2011).

10 Andrew O'Hagan's 'The Satoshi Affair'. *London Review of Books*. June 30, 2016.

11 Satoshi Nakamoto's *Bitcoin: A Peer-to-Peer Electronic Cash System*.

12 Sunny King and Scott Nadal's *PPCoin: Peer-to-Peer Crypto-Currency with Proof-of-Stake*.

13 Joseph Poon and Thaddeus Dryja's *The Bitcoin Lightning Network*.

14 David Schwartz, Noah Youngs, and Arthur Britto's
The Ripple Protocol Consensus Algorithm.

15 The Ethereum 'White Paper'.

16 Best source of historical price data:
www.Bitcoincharts.com

17 The oldest bitcoin forum:
www.Bitcointalk.org

18 For statistics and info on mining and blocks:
www.Blockchain.info

19 A news hub for all things cryptocurrency:
www.coindesk.com

20 Another cryptocurrency news hub
www.cryptocoinsnews.com

21 For more cryptocurrency news:
www.Bitcoinmagazine.com

Glossary

51% Attack In a proof-of-work cryptocurrency such as bitcoin, if an attacker can control 51% of the hashing power on the network, they are technically able to rewrite the blockchain with erroneous information. The difficulty of the proof-of-work is supposed to make achieving this 51% nearly impossible.

ASIC Application Specific Integrated Circuits are devices made for doing only one specific computational task, and are used to bitcoin mining.

Bitcoin The first cryptocurrency, introduced by Satoshi Nakamoto in 2008, and currently the largest cryptocurrency by value in the world.

BitLicense A specific licence for cryptocurrency related businesses in New York State.

Block Each interval of the blockchain is known as a block. They are solved by mining, and write new transactions into the blockchain.

Blockchain The foundation of all current cryptocurrencies, the blockchain is a cryptographically secured ledger, updated to keep track of new transactions. Blockchains can also store other transaction data, not related to cryptocurrencies.

BOINC Berkeley Open Infrastructure for Network Computing is a program that allows sharing resource-intensive computing tasks by breaking them into small pieces and distributing them amongst volunteers across the internet.

Brute-force The only method for most users to try and defeat public-key encryption. It involves guessing at the answer to nearly insurmountable maths equations, until the right answer is reached. The brute-force method is the fundamental activity of proof-of-work cryptocurrency mining.

Byzantine Generals A mathematics problem used to solve problems of fault tolerance in computer systems, and in cryptocurrencies, to create consensus protocols for non-proof-of-work cryptocurrencies.

CAPTCHA Completely Automated Public Turing test to tell Computers and Humans Apart, is a puzzle, typically involving an image and text, embedded in a website to keep bots from flooding a site with spam traffic.

Child DAO When a user decides to leave the DAO, they are placed in a small split-off DAO called a Child DAO.

Correspondent accounts Accounts that banks set up with each other, to swap money back and forth.

CPU Central Processing Unit, the core processor of a computer.

Cryptocurrency A cryptocurrency is a virtual currency that uses cryptography to secure itself, typically within a distributed blockchain.

Cryptography A method of using algorithms to encrypt messages between different parties. It also forms the basis of internet and computer security.

DAO The Distributed, Autonomous Organization, an autonomous corporation set up via Ethereum in 2016, designed to serve as an investment structure. It failed catastrophically in the same year, when a recursive split attack allowed an attacker to drain it of funds.

Dark web A small, isolated version of the internet, set up within the Tor system. There, all servers and visitor requests to those servers are masked by encryption, and nearly impossible to identify.

Difficulty To keep the block length about the same, the cryptocurrency scales up the proof-of-work task, depending on how many computers are producing guess hashes at once. This scaling metric is called the difficulty.

Digital currency A digital currency is a currency that can be expressed in digital format.

Dogecoin The 'joke cryptocurrency', based on an online meme in 2013. Very easy to mine, it has a low value and is often used for games, charity, or online feedback systems.

Ethereum A cryptocurrency network that allows programming to be executed through the blockchain, potentially enabling smart contracts and autonomous corporations.

Fork Derived from when two different developers take the source code of a program into two different irreconcilable directions by making changes to it, it is also the term for odd situations when two different blockchains come into existence on the same network, and the computers of that network must decide between them.

FPGA Field Programmable Gate Arrays are multi-purpose chips that can be custom programmed for specific, computation-intensive tasks.

GPU Graphics Processing Unit, a processor designed to complete many small parallel tasks, such as rendering graphics.

Hash Part of a cryptographic process in which a string of text is converted into a shorter, complex value. If even one character of the original text is changed, the hash is as well. They are used to sign messages cryptographically, and also form a fundamental part of the cryptocurrency mining process.

Hashrate An expression of how much mining is happening on a proof-of-work cryptocurrency network, typically measured in hash per second.

Intermediate nodes Cryptocurrencies that assign a hierarchy to different computers in the network. Above the base users are the intermediate nodes, which have greater authority to authorize transactions and construct the topology of the network.

IP address The unique numbers that identify a particular computer, server, router, or other internet-capable device. They are used as an address system to route data around the internet.

Jed McCaleb Software developer who launched Mt. Gox in 2010, before selling the site to Mark Karpeles.

Lightning Network A suggested means of speeding up the bitcoin blockchain by allowing small, repeating transactions to occur off-blockchain between trusted partners.

Litecoin The primary 'altcoin', often used as alternative to bitcoin. It was released in 2011, and uses a different hashing algorithm called 'scrypt'.

Malware Software specifically designed to do harm to systems for others' gain, such as viruses, exploits, etc.

Mark Karpeles Owner of Mt. Gox, after buying the site from Jed McCaleb in 2013. He was arrested in 2015 and faced charges related to the site's demise.

Masternodes In some intermediate-node cryptocurrencies like Dash, masternodes are computers in the network with a proven stake level. They function to approve transactions and construct the blocks, while other nodes do proof-of-work mining to solve the block.

Mining The act of completing the proof-of-work, in which a computer produces hash guesses in order to solve a new block and add new transactions to the blockchain. Typically, computers solving blocks are rewarded by being transferred some quantity of cryptocurrency.

Mt. Gox The first cryptocurrency exchange that allowed direct purchases of bitcoin and other cryptocurrencies using traditional currency. Founded by Jed McCaleb in 2010, the site was eventually sold to Mark Karpeles in 2013. The biggest exchange until its demise in 2014, the site was often targeted by hackers. The largest theft would be the exchange's undoing, and also landed Karpeles in a Japanese Court on charges of embezzlement.

Point-of-sale terminal The computers commonly used by merchants instead of cash registers, to ring up purchases and charge credit cards.

Pretty Good Privacy Or PGP, one of the first software methods of public-key encryption, created by Phil Zimmerman in 1991 and uploaded to the internet, where users could download it for free.

Proof-of-stake An alternative to proof-of-work, this method adds new blocks to the blockchain by assigning this privilege to computers in the network that control a great deal of the cryptocurrency, judging them to be more trustworthy, as they have more stake in the system.

Proof-of-work The mining activity necessary to produce new blocks in cryptocurrencies like bitcoin. It involves brute-force guessing of hashes, which can then be quickly verified by algorithm.

Public-key encryption Also called asymmetric encryption, this method of cryptography employs public and private keys, so that two parties may exchange encrypted information without ever having to share a codebook.

Ransomware Malware that encrypts the target's computer, and then demands money, typically paid in bitcoins, to decrypt the files again.

Real-Time Gross Settlement Account Also RTGS, a means for banks to move money between them by using a central bank.

Recursive split attack A bug in the DAO that allowed an attacker to request multiple withdrawals at the same time, removing total currency in many multiples of what was held in their account balance.

Ripple A cryptocurrency network designed to allow the international transfer of traditional currencies among banks, service providers, and foreign exchange market makers.

Router A small computer, running a dedicated operating system designed to manage and direct internet traffic across a home, neighbourhood, or region.

Satoshi Nakamoto The pseudonymous inventor of bitcoin. First known to the world in 2008 when he released a whitepaper describing his idea for the cryptocurrency, he disappeared from the internet in 2011. Many people have attempted to determine his real identity.

Segregated Witness A suggested fix to the bitcoin software that would decrease the amount of transaction information stored in the blockchain, speed up transaction confirmation, and potentially fix the transaction malleability problem.

Server A computer on which the files of a website are stored. By responding to requests from users' computers, the server sends these files across the internet, allowing the website to be viewed on the users' computers.

Signature When using a private key to create a cryptographic hash of a message, that hash is called a signature, because only the private key could have made that hash, and using a public key, the signature can be independently verified.

Silk Road A dark web-based marketplace, specializing in illicit goods, namely illegal drugs. Run by the pseudonymous Dread Pirate Roberts, the website was shutdown in 2013 when Ross Ulbricht was arrested and charged with being the founding administrator.

Smart contracts A contract written in programming code, that is able to execute itself given certain specified conditions.

SWIFT Society for Worldwide Interbank Financial Telecommunication, the system that banks use to communicate correspondence account transfers.

Tor Also The Onion Router, a piece of software that allows users to use the internet while obscuring what sites they visit, and their origin point from those sites. It is also used to create the dark web, which is a sort of smaller internet where server locations and site visitors cannot be identified.

Transactions Bitcoin transfers are written as transactions on the blockchain, and are submitted for inclusion in newly solved blocks.

Transaction malleability problem A flaw in bitcoin's software, that enables an improperly formatted transaction to be accepted by the blockchain, then responding with an unexpected transaction ID. If the software is not aware of this unexpected transaction ID, it will often attempt to process the transaction again, resulting in duplicate transactions.

Wallet The private key of a cryptocurrency account. The wallet signs all transactions submitted to the blockchain, and links all the public addresses together.

Virtual currency A virtual currency is a currency that's existence is entirely digital.

Vitalik Buterin The creator of Ethereum.

Illustrations

Figure credits

Figures 5.1, 5.2 and 8.1: www.blockchain.into

Photo credits

Chapter 2
'The identity of bitcoin inventor 'Satoshi Nakamoto' is a mystery': Cultura/REX/Shutterstock
'You don't need physical coins to use bitcoin, but some physical tokens have been created': Sipa Press/REX/Shutterstock

Chapter 3
'The digital privacy tools created by 'cypherpunks' helped give rise to cryptocurrencies': xijian/Getty

Chapter 4
'Public-key encryption keeps online information away from prying eyes': D3Damon/Getty
'The blockchain is the tool that underlies cryptocurrency': alengo/Getty

Chapter 5
'A Chinese bitcoin mine. China is home to the majority of the world's mining pools': Paul Ratje/For *The Washington Post* via Getty
'No picks and shovels: These energy-hungry processers are mining bitcoin': Paul Ratje/For The Washington Post via Getty

Chapter 6
'Not everyone was happy to see Ross Ulbricht, the Silk Road creator, on trial': Spencer Platt/Getty
'Silk Road and many copycat sites were shut down by the US authorities': David Colbran/Alamy Live News

Chapter 7
'Many people lost money with the fall of Mt.Gox': Tomohiro Ohsumi/Bloomberg via Getty

Chapter 8
'Bitcoin ATMs are still a rare sight': Jonathan Raa/NurPhoto/ REX/Shutterstock

'One way to spend cryptocurrency': Mario Tama/Getty

'Will signs like this ever be commonplace?': Sean Gallup/Getty

Chapter 9
'This Roman coin is from around 400 CE, but the first coins were made 300 years earlier': REX/Shutterstock

'In medieval Europe, tally sticks like these were used to record debts and exchanges': By Winchester City Council Museums (Flickr) [CC BY-SA 2.0 (http://creativecommons.org/licenses/ by-sa/2.0)], via Wikimedia Commons

'Golden age: A gold trader at the Bank of England': REX/ Shutterstock

'The days of old-fashioned banks could be numbered': Associated Newspapers/REX/Shutterstock

Chapter 10
'Dorian Nakamoto vehemently denied having anything to do with bitcoin': Jonathan Alcorn/Bloomberg via Getty

Chapter 11
'Is there a fork in the road ahead for bitcoin?': Source/REX/ Shutterstock

'Lightning could save bitcoin': Design Pics Inc/REX/Shutterstock

Chapter 12
'The blockchain could make banks as we know them a thing of the past': Courtesy Everett Collection/REX/Shutterstock

'The technology behind bitcoin is enabling a new solar power network': Lester Lefkowitz/Getty

Chapter 13
Proof-of-work calculations might not be needed for the block-chains of the future': WestEnd61/REX/Shutterstock

'The boardroom of the future?': WestEnd61/REX/Shutterstock

Index